Talking through Reading and Writing

Talking through Reading and Writing

Online Reading Conversation Journals in the Middle School

Daniel Rose and Christine Walsh

ROWMAN & LITTLEFIELD
Lanham • Boulder • New York • London

Published by Rowman & Littlefield
An imprint of The Rowman & Littlefield Publishing Group, Inc.
4501 Forbes Boulevard, Suite 200, Lanham, Maryland 20706
www.rowman.com

6 Tinworth Street, London SE11 5AL, United Kingdom

British Library Cataloguing in Publication Information Available

Library of Congress Cataloging-in-Publication Data

Names: Rose, Daniel, 1976– author. | Walsh, Christine, 1960– author.
Title: Talking through reading and writing : online reading conversation journals in the middle school / Daniel Rose and Christine Walsh.
Description: Lanham, Maryland : Rowman & Littlefield, 2021. | Includes bibliographical references. | Summary: "When readers and writers of all ages are supported socially, emotionally, and academically in their reading and writing processes, they acquire a sense of agency over text, and suddenly they begin to see reading in a different light. They begin to value reading more as a life skill, one that can change the way they act and think, and maybe even change the way they live. The Online Reading Conversation Journal offers teachers a practical teaching tool for creating engaged, independent readers who can make these connections"— Provided by publisher.
Identifiers: LCCN 2020036357 (print) | LCCN 2020036358 (ebook) | ISBN 9781475850901 (cloth) | ISBN 9781475850918 (paperback) | ISBN 9781475850925 (ebook)
Subjects: LCSH: Reading (Middle school) | Reading—Computer assisted instruction.
Classification: LCC LB1632 .R67 2021 (print) | LCC LB1632 (ebook) | DDC 418/.40712—dc23
LC record available at https://lccn.loc.gov/2020036357
LC ebook record available at https://lccn.loc.gov/2020036358

♾ ™ The paper used in this publication meets the minimum requirements of American National Standard for Information Sciences Permanence of Paper for Printed Library Materials, ANSI/NISO Z39.48-1992.

For the readers and writers who come to school with open minds and open hearts, and for the teachers who nurture and guide them.

Contents

Foreword

You know that feeling you get when you enter a bookstore? Your heart beats a little faster as your eyes scan the displays on tables and walls and then settle on book covers that seem to be calling to you, wanting to meet you. That's what happens when I enter Dan Rose's eighth-grade classroom. One does not have to head to a bookcase in a back corner and lean in to read the spines of books to check out titles. His books are standing, waiting to be picked up, or spread out on tables so that entire front covers are visible and accessible. Every side of the room is filled with inviting texts.

I have been in Dan's classroom while supervising student teachers, who tell me they feel like they've discovered a literary paradise. They get daily experience giving book talks, showing book trailers, listening to students' interests so they can match them with appealing books for their independent reading. They read along with the students for ten minutes every class period of every day (well, except for Fridays, when they read more). They witness the relationships Dan has built with the students he has come to know so well through online literary conversations. On days when I supervise, I always bring a book for my student teacher and a book for the cooperating teacher, to add to their classroom libraries. The last time I was in Dan's room, I gave him a nonfiction book about World War II, and he immediately said, "I know six kids who will be fighting over this book." And he could name them.

This book is about the Reading Conversation Journals that Dan uses with his students. But of course this method can only work if it goes hand in hand with a variety of strategies that help students become avid pleasure readers, and many are not when they come to him in September. So consider this foreword as a prequel to the story Dan and Chris are going to tell about authentic student writing and teacher response.

I have also worked with Dan's coauthor, Chris Walsh, in many capacities, so I can say with confidence that she is the most reflective co-learner, researcher, and collaborator he could ever have chosen. Chris and I have been in a writing group with six other women for over twenty years, where she has given astute and nurturing responses to hundreds of drafts. She thrives in classrooms and school buildings at all levels where there are professional development opportunities. And she still works with middle school and high school students. You'll hear her wise and gentle voice in this book as she comments, synthesizes, questions, wonders, and connects aspects of the work Dan and his students have produced. As a philosopher/practitioner, she helps us understand what is happening and consider where we might take things next—in a way that a classroom teacher busy with the continuing work of implementing the online Reading Conversation Journals might not be able to do alone.

While I already knew Dan and Chris, I did not know Dan's students before reading this book. But I sure do now. The honest voices telling their teacher about their current favorite books, their reading practices, aspects of their lives that distract them from reading, their insecurities, their successes, and the changes they see in themselves are clear and compelling. Dan's responses and the ongoing conversations, always building on previous entries, make his classroom come alive. Readers will want to replicate that kind of vibrant reading and writing community.

The rich online dialogues between this teacher and his eighth graders are authentic examples of literary talk. I want to join them, as I would in a book club meeting! The authors' reflections highlight the metacognitive aspects of both student reading and teacher decision-making. Using this model, teachers at all levels could share examples with their students as they establish their own system of journaling about books, reading, and life. The approach leads students to hone their ability to verbalize responses to literature with confidence, and to be aware of their questions, needs, and literary loves.

This book has it all—from the big things, such as educational philosophy, literacy research, and assuring diversity within the classroom library, to the practicalities of determining and recording grades, managing time, mining student data, and corresponding with administrators, colleagues, and families.

A final question in the last chapter asks, "Why isn't this happening in most schools?" I am envisioning that, as a result of *Talking through Reading and Writing* being out in the world, online Reading Conversational Journals *will* be introduced in more and more classrooms. As the authors have shown through multiple examples, writing to a trusted teacher about reading and then receiving personalized feedback will lead to further reading, the ability to verbalize feelings and thoughts, the metacognitive ability to be aware of one's own reading processes, and the utter pleasure of being able to talk to someone else who has read a book that has changed a student's view of the world.

—Sharon Kane, author of
Integrating Literature in the Disciplines

Preface

How We Got Started, or the Birthing of the RCJ

As a teacher of middle-level readers, I think I always instinctively knew that the best way to reach them, the best way to teach them, was through talk. Conversation through conferences.

All the professional books I read talked about the value of talk, the value of the teacher/student conference, the two- or three-minute on-the-fly lesson crafted with each individual student in mind. A short, one-on-one session that had the power to propel literacy students forward and address (with precision) the exact reading and writing skills they lacked or could not demonstrate at that moment. A one-minute, masterful oratory exchange that would mold minds, change lives.

I knew it was the right way to teach readers.

But I was terrible at it.

I tried; I really did. Day after day, year after year, I would take time to sit next to my readers and writers (on a wheeled scooter-like chair) and move around the room with my clipboard taking notes and checking off students, trying to keep conferences to a certain time limit to ensure that I reached everyone in a week, trying to say just the right thing for just the right kid. I did not fail all of the time, just most of the time.

My record-keeping was atrocious during these dark days.

And the behavior of the other students, the ones not involved in the conference, was equally distracting. I found that I was often not fully engaged in the one-on-one conversations I was having, due in part to the attention I was paying the other students who were either talking or getting up out of their seats or asking to go to the restroom or the drinking fountain.

And no one was really talking in the conferences except me. Students would clam up or talk minimally and often so softly I had to lean in and ask them to repeat.

Then there came the day I fell off the wheeled chair and onto the floor.

This was a defining moment for me. I knew, staring up at the tiled ceiling of my classroom from the dusty floor, that there had to be a better way to have richer conversations about reading and writing, conversations that would mold, motivate, and move students forward, make them not only want to read and write, but also want to read and write better. There had to be a more authentic way to determine if growth was really taking place for every student.

There on my classroom floor, among the tiny shavings of pink eraser and number 2 pencil dust, I had an epiphany.

Maybe these masterful conferences didn't have to take place in the overcrowded aisles of my classroom. Maybe, too, there was an easier way to keep track of these conversations, to store them so that teachers could reflect on them, review them for growth and development, use them to make their lessons stronger, more efficient, more productive.

It was time to break free of the rolling stool, the clipboard, the pencil on a leash.

It was time to take back my teaching.

It was time to take these conversations online.

—Daniel Rose

I am an educator who loves talking about, reading about, planning, seeing and implementing good literacy teaching practices. I am passionate about the need for well-planned, student-centered literacy instruction and become inspired when I meet like-minded educators. This is how I met Dan Rose.

As an instructional/literacy coach in Dan's middle school, I have had the pleasure of watching Dan and his students interacting with reading and writing in unique ways—ways that mirror and extend the holistic language-learning theories and practices I've believed in and used as a classroom teacher and in my undergraduate and graduate literacy courses since the 1980s. Once Dan invited me to return to his classroom anytime, I was hooked.

In our inquiry-based professional development course in mindfulness, Dan explored the essential question: *How can I revise my literacy instruction to help create more independent, engaged readers and writers?* Having the opportunity to critically reflect on his teaching practice with a supportive group of colleagues opened the door for something entirely new—the Reading Conversation Journal.

Looking back together on the online conversations Dan had with his students, we were astonished at some of the writing they produced online. We found evidence that students were learning in ways that were not happening in the classroom. The journal offered Dan information about his students and their literacy development that no other method had. The treasure that Dan was sitting on needed to be shared with other teachers.

Dan and I have since learned much from each other by sharing YA books, professional books, and articles about the power of holistic, evidence-based practices in teaching literacy; we've co-authored an article and podcast for NCTE's *Voices from the Middle*; co-presented at local, regional, statewide, and national literacy conferences; and now offer to you our latest writing collaboration and celebration.

I am grateful to have such a dedicated writing and teaching partner.

Happy reading! Happy teaching!

—Christine Walsh

Please note: Every time you read "the teacher" in this book, we are referring to author Daniel Rose, an eighth-grade ELA teacher at Oswego Middle School. We use third person intentionally to make the point that *any* teacher can adapt this method in her classroom to promote independent reading and writing through online conversations with their students.

Please also note that all of the journal excerpts used in this book have been copied verbatim; we have not edited the students' written work in any way. Student names are anonymous.

Acknowledgments

We are thankful, first, to all of our students who come to class each day full of energy, verve, and a sense of wonder and curiosity about books and reading. Without our young readers and their truthful and heartfelt conversations about reading, there would have been no book to write.

Writing this book has been an amazing journey that taught us many things, one of which is that it is okay to rely on others, that we could never accomplish something this big alone. Thanks to our writing group friends and colleagues—Jean Ann, Barbara Beyerbach, Bonita Hampton, Mary Harrell, Sharon Kane, Tania Ramalho, and Bobbi Schnorr—for offering excellent feedback and support throughout the drafting process.

Thanks to Tom, Kira, and Carlie, our editors, for their revision suggestions that strengthened the book. Special thank-yous to Sharon Kane, Barbara Beyerbach, and Alison Anderson for their critical reading of the entire manuscript draft and providing the feedback we needed to move forward.

We appreciate our colleagues—the extraordinary teachers, administrators, staff, and students of the Oswego Middle School, Oswego City School District, and State University of New York at Oswego—who inspire us on a daily basis with their intelligence, vigor, and relentless love of learning and persistent desire to grow and develop intellectually.

To our families for their patience, love, and encouragement during this long, sometimes arduous, book-writing process: for your unceasing support of our passion to write and research and talk about reading and writing and the way young people learn, we are forever grateful.

Finally, a million thank-yous and much love to our biggest cheerleaders, our significant others, Kelly and Brian. You allow us to be the persons we hoped to be.

Introduction

In this book you will read many examples of rich literacy conversations between a teacher and his students that never would have occurred face to face in the classroom. These conversations take place online when eighth graders write to their teacher about the books they are interested in reading and choosing to read. They write about what happens when they read or don't read, how they feel about reading, why they don't have enough time to read, what their reading goals are. And their teacher writes back to them. Every week. What the students reveal about their own literacy development—their successes, their challenges, their growth, their lives—can teach us more about how and what to teach them than any professional book or article can.

The power of these connections moves far beyond just garnering great reading responses. We know that ongoing meaningful connections with adults and with engaging texts bring happier, healthier students to school, students willing to work and explore ideas outside of their comfort zones, students willing to do the more challenging work, students who want to come to school because a teacher is taking the time to get to know them. The social-emotional benefits of the online Reading Conversation Journal are clear and compelling throughout our book.

Teachers who are frustrated about students who choose not to read or choose not to write or have a hard time getting started will find some answers here. Teachers looking for an engaging form of literacy instruction and assessment in reading and writing will embrace this activity and make it their own. All teachers of all grade levels and all content areas can easily implement this idea, as long as their students can read a text (*text* defined broadly) and type on a keyboard. The online Reading Conversation Journal is a vehi-

Introduction

cle for providing for and nurturing the whole student—academically, social-ly, and emotionally.

In part I ("What Online Reading Conversation Journals Are and What They Can Do for Readers, Writers, and Teachers"), we offer basic informa-tion about what the RCJ (Reading Conversation Journal) is, what it is not, its many benefits, and why we believe in this practice. Here we briefly introduce you to Amelia, an eighth grader whose conversations with her teacher we highlight to show their richness and value.

Part II, titled "Motivation, Confidence, and Trust: How Online Reading Conversation Journals Enhance the Teacher-Student Relationship," shows readers how creating supportive, ongoing connections with adolescents through online conversation can build and nurture a positive, trusting rela-tionship. By tracing Kaylee's literacy story, we see the power and potential of these human connections.

In part III ("How Online Reading Conversation Journals Promote 'Uni-verse as Text'"), we bring you into the unlimited world of multiliteracies. Here we introduce you to several different eighth graders whose online jour-nal conversations reveal our need to greatly expand our definition of *text* as we revise our reading instruction.

We titled part IV "How Online Reading Conversation Journals Grow Reading Engagement and Self-Awareness" when we discovered all the ways this literacy activity increases student engagement and helps them become more metacognitive about their reading and about themselves.

Finally, appendix A ("A Dozen Questions Teachers Ask about Using the RCJ as an Integral Part of Their Comprehensive Reading and Writing Pro-gram") is a compilation of twelve questions many teachers ask us as we present the RCJ at local, regional, state, and national conferences. Some questions are practical, nuts-and-bolts-type questions, while others can only be addressed by more thoughtful, in-depth responses. Please write to us at the addresses below and send us your thoughts, successes, challenges, and more questions as you implement and consider the RCJ.

Our goal is to inspire you, our readers—and educators at all levels—to take the time to truly reflect on the importance of setting aside time in the classroom for independent reading and writing, to reflect on the ways you use digital literacy to teach the students of today to read and write. We encourage you to give the RCJ a try and make it your own.

Please write to us and let us know how it goes!

Dan: drose@oswego.org
Chris: christine.walsh@oswego.edu
Website: https://sites.google.com/oswego.edu/roseandwalsh/home

Part I

What Online Reading Conversation Journals Are and What They Can Do for Readers, Writers, and Teachers

I am a teacher at heart, and there are moments in the classroom when I can hardly hold the joy. When my students and I discover uncharted territory to explore, when the pathway out of a thicket opens up before us, when our experience is illuminated by the lightning-life of the mind - then teaching is the finest work I know.—Parker Palmer (1998, p. 1)

Chapter One

The Benefits of Digital Journaling

This book tweaks and then refines the traditional reading conference by taking it online. Instead of conferring side by side with students, whispering our way around the classroom (on rolling chairs or, worse, on our knees or squatting), teachers can utilize an online conferencing platform, responding virtually to each student. Online response journals offer students a place to document feelings, thoughts, and reactions to a variety of texts, while simultaneously providing opportunities to make connections with teachers and think deeply about the materials they read.

There are major benefits to online reading and writing conferences. Here are some of them:

THE LOW-RISK, VIRTUAL ENVIRONMENT

The low risk, virtual environment allows students to elaborate without direct social consequences. Face-to-face conferencing is very effective, but not very efficient. Often, it is difficult to get students to warm up to the idea of articulating thoughts out loud under the looming eyes of the teacher and twenty-five of their closest friends. Just when a student starts to open up a little during a side-by-side talk, valuable classroom minutes have already passed. Add on another couple of minutes to finish the conference, and then multiply that by twenty-five students. A lot of time for very little result.

Students write with more fluency, volume, and frequency when they are asked to write online. They feel free to think and write without the pressure of anyone looking at them or listening to them. They also recognize that they have a caring expert on the other end of the conversation, waiting to read and respond.

STUDENTS ARE MORE ENGAGED

Students are more engaged when working with computers. It's true. Students repeatedly report that they enjoy using technology. It's second nature to them. They love the keyboard and the way their words look neat and clean on the screen, and they love how easy it is to keep track of everything they write. It's natural and authentic.

The online platform allows all students—students with special needs, English Language Learners, and those who struggle to read and write—a level playing field academically, socially, and emotionally. This platform even allows for the exploration of speech-to-text technology for students who need adaptive communication, should the need arise.

TEACHERS CAN BE MORE DELIBERATE AND PRECISE

Teachers can be much more deliberate and precise with their approach to reading and writing instruction. When neither the student nor the teacher is rushed, the ability to respond with careful thought and consideration increases dramatically. Response can arrive not only with more accuracy and thoughtfulness, but also with more depth. Teachers can edit, revise, and even delete written responses to students after careful consideration or upon re-reads. Students feel freer asking for clarification when their peers aren't looking and listening.

This method of careful, thoughtful, deliberate, and micro-tailored instruction is near impossible in traditional face-to-face reading and writing conferences where reactions and responses happen rapidly and in the midst of the moment.

ACCESS TO THE INTERNET

This is the most obvious benefit of online journaling and conferencing. With access to the World Wide Web, the textual universe is at the readers' fingertips. Suddenly, book trailers and book reviews are a click away for readers in search of their next great text. *New York Times* articles about a reader's favorite video game can be there on the screen in front of them in seconds. Teachers no longer have to run around between classes and after school putting together preview stacks for reluctant readers; these stacks become virtual. Book lists, movie previews, music videos, blog posts, audio clips, podcasts—any and all forms of text are in play.

The online conference allows a teacher of reading more flexibility and more creativity to meet students' diverse literacy needs.

EASY RECORD-KEEPING

One of the most difficult aspects of conferencing for teachers and students is keeping track of it all: *What did she say last time we met? What book was she reading? What did I teach last time I was here on my rolling stool? How many times have I conferenced with her in the past month? With whom should my next conference be? Where is my clipboard for notes? How loud should I talk when I am conferencing? What are the other students doing when I am talking to this student? How much more can my knees and back take of squatting and bending up and down all day?*

All of these questions become moot with the online journal. A quick scroll through the response thread will tell instructors everything they need to know before any virtual conference. Plus, there is the added bonus of the student being able to track their thinking and progress not only through a text but also through a reading year. Students can visually see and trace their growth as a reader and thinker from the beginning to the end of the year.

In addition, these student response threads become a fantastic tool at parent-teacher conferences, as well as administrative and team meetings. Teachers are able to copy and paste quotes, lines, and even full student entries into emails to administration, parents, and other area teachers to help illustrate reading progress and motivation through a school year. Formative assessment is ongoing and accessible.

NOT ONLY IS DIFFERENTIATION POSSIBLE, BUT IT ALSO HAPPENS QUITE NATURALLY!

We can differentiate reading instruction for every student in our class as often as we want or need to. Probably the biggest complaint about conferencing is that it takes too much time. There is really no way around this fact.

Often, ELA teachers focus their planning and instruction on the "average literacy student," usually the largest ability group in each class. Other times they find themselves putting a lot of energy into the readers and writers who struggle the most, hoping to raise their skill level and engagement. These approaches cut off opportunities for our most advanced learners, those who are already reading and writing on a high school level and ready for more.

Differentiating reading instruction (i.e., making sure that each reader gets the precise teaching that challenges them at their skill level and nudges them along the reading skill continuum) takes time and effort on the teacher's part. It means listening to each and every student, taking in what they have said, and then figuring out which lesson will help them the most at that particular moment in time while also paying attention to their reading motivation.

Side-by-side conferences get the job done, but at a cost. In a typical reading workshop setting, after a book talk to open a class followed by a multi-minute whole-group reading lesson, ELA teachers are lucky if they get to conference with five or six students during independent reading time before the bell is ringing and the kids are out the door. Then, depending on the grade level, teachers start the whole process over again next class. It is an exhausting cycle.

With the advent of the online journal and conference, each and every student in the class can be reached by the end of the day, week, or whenever the teacher decides that he wants his students to make a new reading response. This type of conferencing also allows teachers the flexibility and time to elaborate on initial ideas and ensure responses are a bit more thoughtful and finely tuned. Since these journals are online, it is possible to respond outside of the classroom, on weekends, away from school, and/or during planning hours.

SOCIAL-EMOTIONAL LEARNING AND THE POWER OF CONNECTION

More than two decades of research shows that social-emotional learning leads to increased academic achievement, improved behavior, and a strong return on investment (CASEL, 2019). When a teacher in middle school or high school takes the time to converse privately with each and every student about a book that student has chosen to read—whether that child is an avid reader, a hater of reading, or somewhere in between—something special happens.

Both teacher and student begin to understand each other better, learn more about each other, and ask each other pointed, sometimes personal questions. After all, don't reading selections reflect the lives and experiences of the reader? Tapping into their academic, social, and emotional needs at such a transitional stage in their lives is crucial for engagement and learning.

Resources on Teaching Social-Emotional Learning (SEL)

Collaborative for Academic, Social, and Emotional Learning (CASEL). (2019). *Collaborative for academic, social, and emotional learning.* www.casel.org

New York State Education Department. (2019). *Student support services: SEL.* www.p12.nysed.gov

Nhat Hanh, T. (2017). *Happy teachers change the world: A guide for cultivating mindfulness in education.* Parallax Press.

The Wallace Foundation. (2017, March). *Navigating SEL from the inside out.* www.wallacefoundation.org

THE VALUE OF FREE AND VOLUNTARY READING

Whether students are destined for college, the workforce, or the military after high school graduation, their time choosing good books, reading them, and talking and writing about them is never wasted. Teachers who cannot find the time in their school week to encourage and facilitate self-selected readings might be surprised as they read this book. It's easier than you think.

Chapter Two

Using a Workshop Model for Reading and Writing

Writing workshop is the method of teaching writing wherein the teacher utilizes daily focused mini-lessons alongside daily independent writing time in conjunction with individualized instruction through one-on-one student writing conferences, a close, careful study and utilization of mentor texts coupled with the study of deliberately crafted teacher-made examples. The goal is always to help create more confident, independent writers.

A Few of Our Favorite Books on Reading/Writing Workshop

Atwell, N. (2014). *In the middle: A lifetime of learning about writing, reading, and adolescents.* Heinemann.

Beers, K. (2012). *Notice and note: Strategies for close reading.* Heinemann.

Calkins, L. (2020). *Teaching writing.* Heinemann.

Calkins, L. (2013). *Units of study for teaching writing.* Heinemann.

Calkins, L. (1994). *The art of teaching writing.* Heinemann.

Gallagher, K. (2011). *Write like this: Teaching real-world writing through modeling and mentor texts.* Stenhouse Publishers.

Gallagher, K., & Kittel, P. (2018). *180 days: Two teachers and the quest to engage and empower adolescents.* Heinemann.

The workshop method has definite advantages for teachers of reading and writing. It is possible, through the workshop method, to see writing improve from day to day and month to month. It is visible. It is clear. Each and every year, in classrooms around the world, student writing gets better, right before teachers' eyes. The students can see the improvements, too, and even articulate and reflect on the differences in their writing after a unit of study—the growth they have made, the confidence they have gained as readers and writers.

Their confidence leads to competence.

Through writing workshops and conferencing, students can cite the numerous, specific ways their writing has improved; they can pick out examples to illustrate these significant changes, and they can explain how the various lessons will help them as they move forward on the writing continuum—into high school, into college, and beyond. Students point to their pages and pages of writing, citing how it has changed, the effect that their writing now has on the audience, the deeper meaning hidden behind the first layer of text. It's all there, in black and white, on the page for the teacher to see.

It is not always as easy to spot reading progress for individual students as it is to see writing improvement. We put our hands and eyes on several examples of student writing samples: writing portfolios, classroom writers' notebooks, written reflections, and first, second, and final drafts for every unit of study. We see specific improvements happening in their use of stronger vocabulary, improved fluency, better word choice, and attention to sentence structure and punctuation.

The reading process, on the other hand, often seems less visible than the writing process, less accessible to the naked eye, less tangible. But the online journal gives teachers a way to build ongoing visual evidence. If you are asking yourself any of the following questions as you teach, perhaps the RCJ is for you and your students: *How am I improving my reading instruction? How am I helping my students to read better? What can I hold in my hands as evidence that my students are all moving forward as readers?*

Most teachers of reading and writing are familiar with the idea of the reading or writing conference—that is, sitting alongside students during workshop time and delivering differentiated, individualized reading and writing instruction based on a student's particular literacy needs at that exact moment in time. This practice has been studied and written about extensively for decades by acclaimed teaching writers from Don Graves and Donald Murray to Nancie Atwell, Lucy Calkins, Bob Probst and Kylene Beers, and Kelly Gallagher and Penny Kittle.

This method of instruction has withstood decades of "new" approaches to the teaching of reading and writing and countless revamps of state and national standards. Conferring survives because it works. It's that simple. It is the best way that teachers of literacy can address the ever-changing needs of each literacy student and the ever-widening gap in literacy skill level among the students in our classes. Teachers cannot expect to stand up in front of the class today and deliver a one-size-fits-all lesson day after day. The classrooms are too diverse for that—with student populations representing an ever-increasing range of abilities in reading, writing, speaking, listening, and viewing.

However, students can show and directly reveal a lot about what they struggle with when reading, what types of texts are easier or more challenging, what makes them think and feel differently. Online conferencing about those metacognitive aspects of reading gets at what is really going on, aspects teachers cannot always capture face to face.

Chapter Three

(The Importance of) Our Core Beliefs

Teaching reading is not supposed to be quick and easy. . . . It's supposed to be about human connection. It's one conversation at a time.—Riff (2017)

The relationship between beliefs about literacy learning and the practice of teaching literacy cannot be overstated. Educators must continue to return to core beliefs again and again. Developing and then revisiting our core beliefs on a regular basis helps teachers become more aware of what it is they believe in and why. What do teachers believe about how students learn to read and write? What conditions best foster the development of literacy skills? Educators need to allow their classroom practices and growing knowledge of student learning, reading, and writing to continually shape, inform, and modify their beliefs. A teacher's core beliefs drive their daily practice. Thinking impacts behavior.

Teachers who are able to articulate clear professional philosophies about teaching and learning make decisions mindfully and continually reflect on what they believe, which in turn, improves practice. Listen to teacher Pernielle Riff talk about her beliefs around teaching and learning literacy in Jennifer Gonzalez's blogpost (see textbox 3.1).

Jennifer Gonzalez's Blogpost and Interview with Seventh-Grade ELA Teacher Pernielle Riff

https://www.cultofpedagogy.com/stop-killing-reading

What do you believe about teaching and learning and, more specifically, about how people learn to read and write? About how people use reading and writing for real purposes and real audiences? Some practicing teachers may have never asked themselves these questions or considered their own answers to these questions.

Considering and articulating beliefs helps instructional leaders who make big decisions about student learning every day come to realize what is valued. Curriculum planning, instruction, and assessment align. Practices are more informed by this way of thinking. For these practitioners, the craft of teaching becomes more meaningful and is raised to a heightened level of professionalism.

One core belief essential to the ideas in this book is that students learn to read better by reading in authentic contexts, and students learn to write better by writing in authentic contexts, through practice and under conditions that generally foster rather than inhibit literacy growth and development. While sitting and observing for hundreds of hours in literacy classrooms, researcher Brian Cambourne (1993) concluded that literacy development occurs optimally when conditions are student-centered, uncomplicated, and barrier-free.

This book also builds on the core belief of integrating reading and writing whenever possible. Reading and writing work hand in hand as two parts of a similar language process. Success in one often leads to success in the other. For many students, reading is the key that unlocks the writing door, and writing becomes the path struggling readers need to crack the reading code. Teaching language arts in tandem also saves precious instructional time and caters to a wider range of learners, abilities, and interests.

While most readers and writers are able to learn to read and write in much the same way they learned to speak, some cannot for a variety of reasons. More direct or intensive instruction may be necessary; lagging skills often need more focused attention. A comprehensive, balanced literacy program is essential for these very reasons. Not all learners learn to read and write in the same way, nor are they all in the same place on the literacy skill continuum when they enter the classroom. Instruction and assessment need to accommodate the needs of all learners. Online reading conversation journals accept each reader/writer where they are—and help them move forward.

Each of these beliefs is supported by solid research in the field, as exemplified by the citations throughout this book.

KNOWING THE READER

I like responding through an online "conversation" with my teacher because it would be harder for him to talk with all of the students 1 on 1. I am able to talk about what books I am currently reading and how I feel about them. It is helping me be more comfortable about talking about books I am reading and it helps me think deeper about what I'm reading.—James

Knowing readers means more than just saying "hello" when they walk through the door at the start of class. Expecting students to respond in deep, meaningful ways to the texts they read means taking time to develop and nurture relationships with readers and writers. Getting kids to work outside of their comfort zones, to push themselves when work gets challenging means taking time to connect with them on many different levels and in many different ways.

Online journals allow teachers a chance to forge these connections. From favorite movies, sports, hobbies, and passions to family life and future goals and aspirations, online journals give teachers the opportunity to converse with all of their students in ways that simply cannot happen during the day-to-day goings-on of the classroom.

WE MUST BE ACTIVE READERS AND WRITERS OURSELVES

Good literacy teachers read. A lot. Books litter our classrooms and desks, take up space on every shelf in our house, pile up on our nightstands, lie propped up in the front seat of our cars. Books congregate in our trunks and backpacks and on our end tables. Articles and magazine subscriptions pile up in our inbox and other electronic folders marked "Podcasts," "Websites," and "Digital Reading." Newspapers and magazines lie folded behind (and under) our computer screens at school and at home. Some teachers read up to seven or eight books at once, alternating between reading for pleasure, for research, for professional improvement, and to expand the ever-growing list of Young Adult titles.

Teachers read as much as they possibly can and then share the texts with students (both the good and the bad), hoping they might read them, too. When teachers share the texts they love, they bring a newfound passion to the lessons they teach.

Good literacy teachers model their thinking about these texts in front of students. They show and share thoughts and questions and ideas so regularly that students can't help but start to take on some of the language and habits and behaviors associated with reading and responding to reading. Literacy teachers talk about and think about and model the kinds of things a reader should notice while reading. They read a sentence/paragraph/page/chapter and then process their thinking aloud, in front of the students. They let students hear what the reader notices and reacts to and explores through reading.

Ask students to design a chart called "What's Worth Noticing in a Text," a chart to help beginning readers start to remember and learn the kinds of things a reader must be alert to as they read/watch/listen to/navigate through a text.

Mostly, though, good teachers of reading practice reading and noticing from a variety of texts. They ask students: What are you noticing as you read? What do you notice about this image? What are you thinking at this point in the video? What is one idea you have at the conclusion of this short film? What did you notice about Taylor Swift's new song? What is one thing you noticed about this Robert Frost poem? What did you notice about this book trailer? What did this Vlogger make you think about? What is this commercial trying to tell you? What did you notice about how reading this changed you?

Many different texts, many different chances to notice things. Regular reading and regular responding is the mantra. In class works better. Not for homework (at least not at first). In class, teachers can watch all students form ideas and ask questions and notice things about a text.

As one student, Kelly, states, "In class I can recognize that other readers are sometimes thinking or noticing or wondering the same thing I am and sometimes I am the only reader who noticed something. Sometimes I even noticed the same things as the teacher and this instills a sense of confidence." Train literacy students to be the constant observer, always on the lookout, allowing curiosity to surface, always noticing things. It is only after readers begin to notice that they begin to wonder about books, about movies, and about the world around them and their place in it.

PROVIDE READERS WITH CHOICE

> I'm reading *The Deathly Hallows* right now and I plan on finishing it by the end of this month or by the beginning of next month. After I finish this series I plan on reading *The Maze Runner* series. For the rest of the year I definitely want to find something new and different to read, I'm just not sure what. I'd be glad to hear some of your suggestions!—Sydney

In many classrooms, students can choose what they read and what they respond to and sometimes even how to respond. Without motivated readers, teachers cannot hope to support the sort of student who will leave the class-room ready to use reading as a means of learning, self-discovery, and growth. Motivation happens first through choice in reading material. Adult readers choose virtually everything they read—from the golf magazine at the barber shop to the online cooking recipe for "famous meatloaf" to be replicated for dinner. Perhaps most importantly, if adults don't want to read something, they don't.

PROVIDE TIME FOR CLASSROOM READING AND WRITING

> I am finding Reading Fridays beneficial because it's the only time I get to read. Yes, it's pretty hard to find time after, before, and on the weekends. I'm very busy with hockey, certain clubs, and homework. At home I would be doing other things I just don't think I have the time to—actually finish a book. What frustrates me the most is that I can't find a book that I'm into so that's annoying. The most difficult thing is finding a book.—Kim

Readers get better at reading by reading, just as students learn to write better by writing. Spending time during the school day actually reading and writing is worthwhile and builds muscle memory and stamina, especially when a trained professional is on the other end reading, assessing, and giving on-the-spot feedback, inviting the reader/writer to delve deeper into the text and into their response to it. Teachers should never feel guilty about providing sustained, silent, free-choice reading time.

Chapter Four

Meet Amelia

Amelia is a student who, without too much effort, glides through school with high grades and top test scores. She is quiet and reserved in class, participates only when called on, and does her work without complaint, without fuss, day in and day out. Before the online Reading Conversation Journal, Amelia and more advanced literacy students like her would coast through English class. Although teachers often leave the door open for students to challenge themselves and push themselves as readers and writers, students like Amelia often do the assigned work and nothing more.

Teachers want all students to push themselves beyond what is expected and are frustrated when top students submit work that is average or just meets the requirements. Through the conversation journal, teachers will be able to nudge students forward, pushing them past their comfort zone and well beyond what they think they are capable of.

Take note of Amelia's conversation as she reads and responds to *Silence of the Lambs*, a dialogue that spans about two months and illuminates our core beliefs as they apply to practice:

Teacher: How is Silence of the Lambs going? I know it is a lengthy book! I like your observation that the book "messes with" your head. What do you mean by that? How can a writer mess with a reader's head? Why would they want to? What benefit does it serve the story? How could this possibly make the reading experience more entertaining or enjoyable?

Amelia: Sadly, I haven't been able to read as much as I normally do. I was at a big swim meet all weekend, so I didn't have time. That doesn't mean the book is any less interesting. When I said the Silence of the Lambs "messes with your head," I meant it's hard for some (most) people to believe that humanity is capable of things like that. . . . The author might want to make their book have a lasting impression, and that's one way to do it. It could also symbolize an experience they went through, like maybe someone close to them was murdered a similar way, and they wanted to try to understand why/how someone could do that to another person. Books like the Silence of the Lambs are entertaining and enjoyable to read because they are full of suspense.

Teacher: How did the (swim) meet go? In what style do you swim? Let me know how you are progressing with Silence of the Lambs.

Amelia: The meet went good. It was supposed to be the last championship meet of the short course season (25 yard pools), but I qualified in the 100 backstroke for the Eastern Zone team. The Zone meet is Friday (3/30/18). I just read a disturbing part in the Silence of the Lambs. It was Starling's first time photographing a dead body, and Thomas Harris didn't leave a single detail out. In this part, Starling is making rapid progress at her job, and her and Crawford are waiting for the fingerprints of the dead lady to process.

Teacher: Awesome, Amelia!!! Oh, boy. I remember this part. Stuck in my head FOREVER!!!!

How is the book going? How is swimming? Are you nervous for tomorrow? Are you just swimming the backstroke or are you involved in other races? Will you bring your book with you and try to read on the trip to and from the meet lol? What do you think we can learn from a book like the Silence of the Lambs?

Amelia: I am still on the part where Starling and Crawford are obsessing about the insect or moth that was found in the victim's throat. I wonder what is so important about that moth. So far, three chapters in a row have been completely about the process of identifying the moth. What if the type of moth it is relates to the type of person Buffalo Bill is? Maybe, Buffalo Bill is scared (or was scared) of moths. It could have something to do with his stressor, which is what made his mind snap to become a serial killer.

Teacher: This book is so good. I can't even believe sometimes that people think these things up. Amazing!! How did the swimming go? Anyway, the whole moth thing. So interesting. I remember this part very vividly, when they tweeze the moth out of the victim's mouth—that part is forever stuck in my head. Can't ever get it out. When a writer spends a lot of time on one thing, they obviously want you to think deeper about it. If I remember right, this is the thing that helps them figure it out. Right? You are on to something!! What kind of moth was it? Did it say? Maybe that's important, ya know? Like certain moths are known to do (or represent) certain things in certain cultures or something. I don't know. Have you ever done some quick research while you are reading a book? HMMMMMMM. Maybe you can try it for this book. What variety of moth was it?

Amelia: Due to State Testing, I am a good half way through the book now. When I get home tonight I want to read about 50 pages before swim practice, then after I want to watch the movie, just because it's Friday the 13th. The Zone meet went good, considering I was sick or had orchestra for the two weeks leading up to it. Yes, I think the moth is helping them figure it out. The book said the moth was a Erebus odora. I just looked it up, and it's nickname is "the Black Witch Moth." I also found that in Mexico and Hawaii, it is associated with death. Mexico has a much darker view of the moth, since the time of the Aztecs it has been known as mariposa de la muerte, which means "butterfly of death." It is believed that the moth will appear when someone dies. In Hawaii, the presence of the moth is viewed as the soul of a recently dead person coming to say a final goodbye. However, in Texas and the Bahamas, the moth is a sign of good luck. Before this, I've never done quick research while reading a book.

Teacher: Great!!! How do you think quick research (like what you did on the moth) can help a reader? What does it do for a reader? The title (Silence of the Lambs) is very interesting. I wonder if you could do some quick research on the lamb (the animal) and see what you can find and how it relates or interconnects with the text.

Amelia: The quick research I did on my last entry about the moth helped me a lot. Now, I'll see how many times the moth comes up, and how Thomas Harris uses it in the text. I quickly looked up what lambs are supposed to represent in the Silence of the Lambs, and I found that Clarice stayed with relatives when she was younger and heard lambs screaming before being slaughtered. She even tried to save one and run away with it, but the plan failed. As an adult, she has been haunted by nightmares of screaming lambs. The lamb is a common symbol of innocence and sacrifice. In the book, the Senator's daughter (the one that has been kidnapped) is the lamb. As Clarice goes on a quest to save her, she gradually redeems her own sense of power, the power to be strong, to be effective, and to save others. As she does, the screaming lambs in her head stop.

This example highlights the importance of each of our core beliefs regarding quality literacy instruction. First, it shows how a teacher's intimate knowledge of his students allows for deeper personal connections and can help encourage readers to use a variety of texts to make meaning. It points to this teacher's direct modeling of the reading/writing process, belief in student choice in their voluntary reading, and a steadfast commitment to devote time each and every Friday when students can take a breath, pick a good book, curl up and read in a low-pressure situation, and then have a conversation about what they are thinking and feeling. Wow.

What other method of instruction can accomplish this much?

FINAL THOUGHTS

Middle school students often comment about how they *used to read* or that they remember reading *all the time* in third and fourth grades, how they used to enjoy books. The research is indisputable. Independent reading is a powerful force in moving a literacy student along the reading continuum and thus preparing them for a successful (and meaningful) life inside and outside the classroom walls. Yet many teachers rarely find time or engaging ways to incorporate this into their literacy curriculum, instruction and assessment. Stephen Krashen, author of *Free Voluntary Reading* (2011) and longtime advocate for free voluntary reading in schools, writes,

> Children can make rapid progress in reading under the right conditions. It's never too late to become a good reader. So instead of worrying about at what age your children learn to read, focus on getting them hooked on books. In fact, get them addicted to reading. (Krashen, 2019)

When readers are supported socially and emotionally in their reading and writing processes, they acquire a sense of agency over text, and suddenly they begin to see reading in a different light. They begin to seek and experience pleasure through reading, and they begin to value reading more as a life skill, one that can change the way they act and think, and maybe even change the way they live.

Part II

Motivation, Confidence, and Trust: How Online Reading Conversation Journals Enhance the Teacher-Student Relationship

Good teachers join self and subjects and students in the fabric of life. . . . Good teachers possess a capacity for connectedness.—Parker Palmer (1998, p. 11)

Chapter Five

Meet Kaylee

This part of our book asks readers to consider the importance of the affective domain in teaching and learning: engaging adolescents and establishing rapport as a foundational piece of teaching English Language Arts. As a positive, supportive relationship is established and grows, teachers and their students begin developing a mutual confidence and trust that motivates and nurtures that relationship through conversation. Young readers and writers today need a variety of literacy skills to navigate the complex world in which they live, and they need capable, trusted adults to help guide them. Attention to the whole child—including their social-emotional learning—is at the heart of the Reading Conversation Journal. Authentic conversation threads with eighth graders exemplify these ideas.

Definitions of Affective Domain

- The affective domain includes factors such as student motivation, emotions, attitudes, perceptions, and values. Teachers can increase their effectiveness by considering the affective domain in planning courses, delivering lectures and activities, and assessing student learning. (https://serc.carleton.edu/NAGTWorkshops/affective/index.html)
- The affective domain describes learning objectives that emphasize a feeling tone, an emotion, or a degree of acceptance or rejection (Krathwohl et al., 1964), as opposed to the cognitive domain, which focuses on thinking skills such as analysis, evaluation, and synthesis.

> We believe both are necessary components of effective literacy in-
> struction, but without the affective focus, cognitive engagement can
> be difficult.

Kaylee is the prototypical middle school student. When asked about her
reading habits, she admits that she does not consider herself a reader and that
she finds books boring or not worth the effort. Kaylee says that there was a
time when she enjoyed reading back in elementary school, but at some point
over the past few years, books have taken a backseat to homework, late-night
basketball practices, and social media. Kaylee will admit that she could see
herself reading again if she had the time and the right book, but books are not
usually the thing she turns to when she has free time outside of school.

When asked to recall how many books she has read on her own over the
past two years, Kaylee says "zero" (but does add that she has read five or six
class books whereby the teacher reads the book out loud or plays the audio
for the class). With the addition of just ten minutes of daily reading time, we
notice a significant change in Kaylee's attitude about reading. In her September RCJ entry below, we can already see increased motivation in Kaylee and
a desire to want to read more on her own.

Kaylee: I am currently reading *The Graduation of Jake Moon*. In this
book the character Jake Moon is fighting with the fact that his grandfather's Alzheimer's is controlling his life. Whatever or whenever he tries
to do something new, his after school "job" always gets to him. He has
lost friends, stopped trying out for news things, and right now, he's in
trouble with his mom. Me as a reader I like to read to myself, I'm kind of
a slow reader but I love to read, only if it's a book I'm into. *The Graduation of Jake Moon* is a fantastic book and I am completely into it and
cannot wait to find out what happens at his graduation.

Teacher: I am so happy to hear that you are enjoying this book. Barbara
Park is one of my favorite authors. If you have not read *Mick Harte Was
Here* yet, please read that book next! It is also a WONDERFUL read. I'm
so glad that you take your time while you read, Kaylee. I bet you don't
read slowly all of the time. I would bet that you take extra care when you
come to an exciting moment, or a moment full of tension, or a sad moment. That is what great readers do—they read quickly or slowly or
mediumly (not a word!) when they need to, or when the writing tells them
to. Let me know what you think of the ending of *Jake Moon*! Looking
forward to hearing from you soon.

Kaylee's September entry is typical in some ways, but unique in others.
Most eighth graders will admit that independent reading is easier (and more

enjoyable) if they have a book that they like and that they want to read. In talking with more than one thousand seventh and eighth graders through the years, it seems that pleasure reading, choice reading, takes a backseat to other more teacher-centered reading after about the fourth grade. Middle-level students say that this is due to the heavier curriculum (and homework) load associated with middle school, coupled with extracurricular activities like clubs, sports, music lessons, and dance lessons, not to mention the allure of cell phones and video games.

There are so many reasons to choose not to read. This is why giving students regular reading time might be one of the most crucial implementations a teacher can provide.

For the very first RCJ entry of the year, teachers might work with a prompt asking students to tell which book they selected to read first and what is happening in that book. Students could be asked to tell all about themselves as readers: What kind of a reader are you? Do you consider yourself a "big" reader? What was independent reading like last year? In elementary school?

In September, teachers should set the stage for a year of conversation, and so it is okay at this point to give a premade prompt to get students rolling. As the year progresses, and students become accustomed to the RCJ, responses will become more organic, written with the needs of each individual learner in mind.

How essential is daily independent reading time to students (and teachers) adapting this conversation journal? So essential that we argue for at least ten minutes a day, every day, no exceptions.

Ten minutes. Every day. No exceptions.

This might be a significant change, especially for teachers working with class periods that are a measly forty-three minutes long (or less). Ten minutes become even more significant.

But wait. We know what you're thinking.

Allowing students to read in class is not really teaching, right? Kids are just . . . reading. There is no real learning happening during that reading time, and surely, there is no real teaching happening.

Students should be taking notes and analyzing text, exploring new vocabulary, testing theories, comparing, contrasting. Students should be conducting experiments, formulating new ideas about the world and their place in it; they should be conversing about the Cold War, debating the decisions of our policyholders; they should be collecting facts and information on Galileo and Bill Gates and Harriet Tubman.

Students should be evaluating the world from different perspectives, finding out where they fit in, where they belong. Students should be predicting and connecting and deciphering and decoding and implementing and exchanging and devising and correlating. Students should be using the information in front of them to grow and prosper, to make the world a better, more peaceful place. Students should be exploring and creating and learning and building new ideas on their own and at their own pace. Right?

Good news.

This is all happening when they read on their own with a book of their choosing. Regular reading time is at the core of the RCJ—the responses, the conversations, the connections, the confidence, the motivation, the risk-taking, the courage. These precious daily reading minutes lead to an entire year of teaching and learning and growth. The instruction happens organically, too; it's not forced on the student. The conversations (the reading and writing instruction) happen at the optimal pace for that particular student, in a low-risk environment with a book that they selected and love.

Krashen (2003) makes the claim that free voluntary reading "may be the most powerful educational tool in language education."

Additional Stephen Krashen Publications on the Value and Benefits of Free, Voluntary, and Independent Reading

- Free voluntary reading (FVR) results in better reading comprehension, writing style, vocabulary, spelling, and grammatical development. (https://www.azquotes.com/quote/1344980)
- Free voluntary reading is the reading of any book (newspaper, magazine, comic, or text) that students have chosen for themselves and is not subject to follow-up work such as comprehension questions or a summary. It serves to increase literacy and develop vocabulary. (http://esl.fis.edu/teachers/support/krashen.htm)
- Stephen Krashen's blog that comments on the importance of books and libraries, especially for children of poverty. (http://skrashen. blogspot.com/2018)

The RCJ is a place where students can recall information from the books that they are reading and reflect on their successes and failures during the process of reading and making meaning from text. The way a student responds in the RCJ (at first) is not as important as their willingness to respond, to write something. In this next entry, we follow Kaylee's thinking in her journal as she recalls key moments from her book. It is clear from this entry that Kaylee has a good handle on the plot and sequence of action occurring in *Jake Moon*.

Kaylee: I am still finishing the book *The Graduation of Jake Moon*. Jake has gone to the pancake house with his family willingly and his mother asked him to take his grandfather to the restroom to wash his hands off, when he comes back he is rushing to his mother trying not to be seen, when he sees two girls at the pancake house, he ignores them. His grandfather who was just with him has now sat down with a lady and yelled "Scat!" That's when he got so embarrassed he left and started walking home. His mom drives and finds him and holds traffic up while Jake refuses to get in the car. He runs through a store and a fence to get away and sits down by a trash bin with his head down. Then Mrs. Russell shows up. After their conversation Jake comes home and sits with his grandfather on his porch, that's all I've read in *The Graduation of Jake Moon* so far.

Teacher: I think I saw that you finished this book, right? What did you think of the book overall? What did you like most about the book, Kaylee? Have you ever read another book like *Jake Moon*? Is that the first book you have finished this year? How do you like having at least 10 minutes of independent reading time in class EVERY DAY this year? Do you think it is helping you as a reader? As a student? How many books do you think you will finish on your own this year, knowing that you will have that much reading time in class every day?

What should a teacher be doing during the ten minutes of silent, choice reading?

Well, reading, of course!

Stand up, right in front of the class, fan the book open proudly with your eyes moving back and forth across the page. Throughout the school year (especially early on), teachers adapting the RCJ can establish themselves as serious readers—prove to their students that they don't just teach and talk about reading. Teachers can show their students that they live reading.

"Do not bother me during reading time!" teachers might warn in September. "You better have a good reason for coming up here during my reading time! How could you forget your book in your locker? I can't wait to read today! I am at such a pivotal moment in this story!"

There will be no faking this enthusiasm for the written word. Teachers, too, will be reading from books that they love, not only for the joys associated with reading a great story, but also for the teaching and learning possibilities that weave themselves throughout the pages of a well-penned text. There is so much power and beauty in seeing students absorbed in a great book. It is the fuel that feeds the reading teacher's fire.

Teachers might start class by saying, "Everyone hold their book up high in the air. Look up at your book. Study the cover. Think about what happened the last time you read. Think about what made you want to pick up that particular book. Why did you check that book out of the library? What made you want to read it? Each book you pick up should be carefully considered.

Books don't randomly appear on teachers' desks or nightstands. They are selected very deliberately."

Every book a student tries out should have a selection story, a story about how the book came to be in the reader's hands, how the book was chosen. When students share the story behind how a book was selected, they are offering valuable information that can help a teacher understand the process by which a particular reader settles on a text to read. Are students benefiting from classroom book talks and online book lists? Are they struggling to find strategies to pick great books? The faster students can learn to find great books, the faster they can fall in love with reading.

And teachers might want to share their book selection stories, too.

We might stand in front of the class with a copy of Robert Cormier's *I Am the Cheese* and explain that we are reading the book for the third time ("Why would you read a book three times!?" the students will shout). We can tell the selection story of that book, talk about how we first read a Cormier book called *The Chocolate War* and loved it. We will recount how Cormier's writing style—mysterious and dark, and sometimes funny—fits us well. We can fill them in on our other experiences with *I Am the Cheese*, how the book is like a puzzle, a Rubik's Cube waiting to be solved. "It's a psychological thriller that is like a jigsaw puzzle," we might say. "Each page is like another piece of the puzzle, and only when you arrive at the final page does a clearer picture emerge."

We can tell students how a book can be different the second or third time through. That readers can experience books in different ways at different ages. We might urge them to reread a "childhood favorite."

Then, students (and teacher) can sit still and read for ten minutes from their choice book.

During the ten minutes, teachers might look up from the page and find a few eyes on them. Students are curious, especially in September. They will want to know if their teacher is taking this time (and reading) seriously. They will want (and need) to know what a real reader looks like. As a result of teacher modeling, students will start to hold their books out in front of their faces (like the teacher), sit up straight with both hands on the book (like the teacher), smile, laugh, and gasp at appropriate parts of the book (like the teacher), groan when they have to stop reading (like the teacher). Oh, and by the way, you can expect all copies of *The Chocolate War* and *I Am the Cheese* to be checked out of the library by the end of the day.

This very well may be the first time all day that these students (and teachers) have actually slowed down, taken a breath, and focused in silently on one particular activity. These ten minutes can be mood altering for sure, maybe even life altering. Eighth-grade students comment all the time about the calming effect of reading time during what can be stressful, fast-paced days.

Spying on readers means knowing what they are reading, how much they are reading, when they are reading, and how far along they are in their book. It also might mean checking in with them during reading time if they start to look disengaged from the text.

Kaylee's teacher knows when she has finished *The Graduation of Jake Moon* because he can see her reading every day in class; he will have checked in with her every day during the ten minutes and talked with her via her RCJ in depth once a week for the entire month of September. Kaylee's teacher has also chatted with her in the halls, at the start of class, and during study hall. Reading has become an integral part of Kaylee's classroom routine and an integral part of Kaylee's life.

Kaylee: I have finished *The Graduation of Jake Moon*. It is a great fit for me, I love how he understands his grandfather's disease. But it's like he just doesn't want to. This book is the first book I've read, and finished this year. It was a great book and makes me want to read more like this. Now, I am reading *Mick Harte was Here*. This book makes me think about my home, how would I handle losing my only real brother? How would it affect my life? Would I still be in shock, or will I cry until I can't breathe? It really makes you wonder, even though I'm only 27 pages into the book, I have already made a connection to the character, Phoebe.

Let's take an opportunity to thank authors like Barbara Park. Many readers are familiar with Park's hugely popular Junie B. Jones series and Junie's bold, hilarious, and sometimes sneaky and inappropriate ways of looking at the world. Teachers might not be so familiar with some of Park's books written for older kids, though, books like *Skinny Bones*, *The Kid in the Red Jacket*, *Don't Make Me Smile*, *Operation Dump the Chump*, and especially *Mick Harte Was Here* and *The Graduation of Jake Moon*.

Like most eighth graders, Kaylee came into the classroom with low reading stamina: the ability of a reader to push through a book, the ability of a reader to start and finish a book (even when the reading gets tough)—to persevere. To maintain reading focus for longer and longer periods of time.

How can a teacher tell when a student has low reading stamina? Tell-tale signs of low reading stamina include: constant book swaps, three or more trips to the library in one week, an inability to sit and read for the full ten minutes (getting up for a tissue or drink or to throw something away, doing other homework during reading time), complaints that reading is boring or stupid, "forgetting" to bring a book to class, or—the most popular sign of low reading stamina in eighth grade—consistently and repeatedly abandoning books after thirty or forty pages with the excuse that the book came to a "slow part."

These low-stamina signs are much more evident during the first few weeks of school, and it is clear that most eighth graders are not used to any sort of extended reading time (beyond three or four minutes). Teachers can expect reading stamina to improve quickly after implementing ten minutes of regular reading time.

YouTube Video and Definition to Help Teach Your Students about Reading Stamina

- https://www.youtube.com/watch?v=CzTQD15WBCw
- "Reading stamina is a child's ability to focus and read independently for longer periods of time without being distracted or without distracting others" (Reading Rockets, 2012).

Many elementary schools allow students some sort of monitored, choice reading time. Whether that means thirty minutes, fifty minutes, or ninety minutes, it is universally known that students are likely getting a chance to read by themselves every day in the elementary grades. Who knows why a shift occurs in the middle and high school years? Students are not too clear on this either, but what is clear is that choice, independent reading seems to take a backseat to classroom reading and reading with "strings attached."

At best, independent reading at the secondary level might be assigned for homework or squeezed in on the days before long breaks. Even if students are allowed to select their own books at the secondary level, there always seems to be something to go along with the reading: a book report, a presentation, a summary.

Reading for pleasure, it seems, is forgotten, an activity reserved for only the most dedicated, passionate readers who are usually the best students, which means that learners in most dire need of discovering the joy and pleasure in reading may not have the chance (or time) to start and finish a book of their choosing during their secondary years.

Students like Kaylee, students who have lost some of the passion for reading (along with some of their reading stamina), are the perfect candidates for a book like *Mick Harte Was Here*. It can become a go-to book at the start of the year for students who love realistic fiction and need to be reminded of the feelings associated with finishing a book. *Mick Harte* is intense, it's real, it stirs emotion, it's funny, and the protagonist, Phoebe, speaks with a candor and depth of feeling that is immediate and long lasting.

Kaylee says it best when she says that after twenty-seven pages she has already "made a connection with Phoebe." Teachers will make that same connection after page 1!

In addition, the book is short.

Mick Harte is under a hundred pages long and provides an opportunity for a middle-level reader to get through an entire book at a time in their schooling when reading (for enjoyment and pleasure) has been pushed to the back of the closet. When students feel the accomplishment of finishing a book early in the year, it's like a magic potion. The confidence level rises, and so does the interest in reading. Never underestimate the power of a short (great) book!

List of Great Short Middle-Level Titles That Build Confidence to Start the School Year

1. *Mick Harte Was Here* by Barbara Park
2. *Junie B. Jones* by Barbara Park
3. *The Graduation of Jake Moon* by Barbara Park
4. *One Crazy Summer* by Rita Williams Garcia
5. *Tuck Everlasting* by Natalie Babbitt
6. *Crossover* by Kwame Alexander

After finishing *Mick Harte*, Kaylee goes on to finish three more books by February and then completes her fourth by the end of March. Her fourth book, *Touching Spirit Bear* (by Ben Mikaelsen), was another piece of realistic fiction that she picked out all on her own.

Oh and, by the way, *Touching Spirit Bear* is 324 pages long.

Chapter Six

Nurturing the Relationship

One way teachers can foster more efficient, more meaningful learning in the classroom is by first cultivating and nurturing student–teacher relationships early on in the year. The Reading Conversation Journal, then, becomes a much-coveted opportunity for teachers to establish and build on the kind of meaningful relationships that will make a student want to grow academically, socially, and emotionally.

The secondary school day, as we have already seen, offers teachers very little chance to connect with each and every student with whom we come into contact. Yes, teachers can use class time to share life stories with their students, but not every story is the right story for every kid. And there is curriculum to teach and ten minutes of reading and . . . you get the idea. Time is short!

The RCJ offers a place to connect with every student, once a week (or more if a teacher so chooses). A place to laugh with students, a place to cry, a place to wonder or rant, a place to show how life and reading intersect. A place where teachers can show how they are human, too. A place where we can offer students another side of ourselves, and where we can learn so much more about them.

Teacher: Hi Kaylee! Besides talking about books, what do you spend most of your time doing outside of school? Do you have anything about which you are truly passionate? Do you have a favorite band or artist? Favorite song? What do you do with yourself when you have time off from school? What would a perfect day look like for you? Looking forward to reading your answer!!

Kaylee: Other than books, my perfect day would be waking up nice and early to start my day, getting up and ready to go to my grandparents to say hello and go outside to their woods to explore the trails. I would get my mud boots and step in every muddy, wet spot off the trails all alone with a large stick to walk around with. I've always loved doing that, not having to listen to the chatter of younger or older siblings of mine, just the chatter of birds and the trees. Then when I go back to my nana and papa's house, I will make hot chocolate and sit in the kitchen and watch the birds come to the bird feeder by the window. I love listening to any upbeat songs, that will get you going and pumped up. Normally when I go out to my nana's house I always ride the four wheeler, now that I have a new puppy Lady, I have been taking time from what I like to do to make sure she has the best life a little puppy would want. With her owner, me and my little sister, we always go to their backyard and run around wild. Lady always catches us. It's the most fun I've had in a long time. I love it.

Teacher: Right before school started this year, we had to put our 16 year old pug named Gary down. I hate saying that—'put the dog down.' It does not seem right, ya know? It was one of the worst days of my life—the day I decided to let Gary go (that sounds a little better).

Anyway, my kids are asking for a new dog—they want a puppy, and they are constantly showing me pictures of these very cute puppies, trying to get me to cave. But I find myself getting a little angry when they show me the pictures. I'm not sure why. Like I expect them to be more upset about Gary or something. Kind of like Phoebe in Mick Hart Was Here. Like she is having all these complicated emotions about Mick. That's how I feel about Gary, too.

If teachers expect students to write in real and open and honest ways about learning and reading and life (and all the emotion, frustration, joy, and confusion that go along with it), then teachers might learn to be open and honest and real about their own lives, their own learning, and how it's all connected to their reading.

Because let's face it: what we read reflects how we live.

Stock brokers read financial magazines and online articles about ticker symbols and expense ratios and Roth IRAs; mechanics read intricate manuals about cars and engines, browse websites and videos dedicated to car maintenance, and read about new innovations in steel and replacement parts; new parents gobble up all the information they can on paper or screen about what to expect during the first few months with a newborn; and yes, teachers read all there is to know about literacy learning and brain development and teaching methods and best practice.

Reading forever intersects with life.

So, when Kaylee's teacher asks her (early on in the year) to describe her perfect day, he is seeking a glimpse into her life, a glimpse that will intersect and intermingle with everything they read. Without really knowing it, Kaylee is providing crucial information her teacher needs to help her along the path to lifelong reading. She is providing the information her teacher needs to help her find the kinds of books that will propel her forward in her reading life.

Through her simple but beautifully written response, Kaylee's teacher learns so much about her: her deep connection with her grandparents, her love of the outdoors, her introspective nature, her silly and playful personality, her love of animals and music and hot chocolate, and her ability to appreciate the beauty of nature and the sounds that accompany it. Kaylee also reveals that she has siblings and a new dog, and that she likes to play, run, and be active.

Based on this thoughtful response from Kaylee, her teacher can start gathering book titles that might fit her as a reader.

Five, ten, fifteen titles should come to mind: YA titles (and adult novels) that would fit Kaylee's personality and passions, fiction (and nonfiction) titles that would make her want to read through the night, on weekends, holidays, in the waiting room at the dentist's office. The more books her teacher reads, the more recommendations he will have at her fingertips.

If her teacher can't think of book titles for Kaylee, can't make many recommendations, it will be near impossible to get her hooked on reading. But teachers should not worry too much if they have not logged many Young Adult novel reading hours; titles for Kaylee are (thankfully) just a click or two away. Teachers only need to perform a quick Google search using phrases like "YA Nature Fiction" or "YA Outdoors Fiction" or "YA Survival Fiction."

It is worth mentioning here that teachers can talk more meaningfully and more passionately about books after having read them. To build trust and motivation in readers, to make them want to sit still with a book for ten minutes *every* day, teachers can learn to be honest and open, vulnerable even, which might mean sharing some stories from their own lives.

When Kaylee reads the story of the loss of her teacher's dog and the connection to the protagonist's feelings in *Mick Harte Was Here*, she is learning about the way books and life overlap, how books can bring clarity to readers in times of trouble, in times of loneliness. Entries like this one work to build a shared trust, a teacher–student relationship that will be nurtured throughout the school year.

This is one of the greatest reading lessons that can be taught through the conversation journal: that books can be a way to a more meaningful, more powerful, more rewarding life, if we allow books to lead us.

If we learn to let books take us by the hand.

Chapter Seven

Playing with Language

That reading and writing reinforce each other is undeniable, and so the RCJ also serves as a useful tool to address and develop lasting writing skills tailored to the needs of the student. The freedom and low-risk nature of the RCJ allows students to take risks in their writing and thinking without fear of being graded or judged.

There is an added bonus, too: each of the teacher's responses (back to the student) serve as mentor texts for responding readers who learn (by example) to use similar content vocabulary, spacing, sentence structure techniques, punctuation and grammar, and questioning. When readers like Kaylee recognize that they have a captive audience, and that their writing is having an effect on that audience, they begin to understand the power of writing (yes, even response writing!).

Kaylee: I got another puppy, four dogs incount. He's a blue heeler, his name is Loki, like the god of mischief. The name suits him. Anyways, I'm almost done with my book, after this I'm going to read a different book I've already picked out, really excited. I've been waiting to read this book ever since it just appeared next to my seat one day, like it was put there as a sign, the sign saying in big, bold, neon print "PICK ME." my book *Mick Harte Was Here*. Is one of the best (and one of the only) books I've actually read fully. Excited for this ending, maybe Phoebe will finally understand that she has to 'let Mick go', see what I did there Mr. Rose??

Teacher: First of all—I am really glad that you finished *Mick Harte*. It is one of my favorite books, ever. This new book sounds interesting. Do you think you will finish this book, too? How did you find it? What about

Mick Harte did you like so much? What made *Mick Harte* one of "the only books you have ever finished"?

The conversation journal gives students a consistent chance to develop their reading and writing skills, as Kaylee so beautifully illustrates in this entry. This venue pushes students to play with writing topic choice, vocabulary, and punctuation, and to test and build different organizational patterns and structure in their writing. The RCJ also creates a space where students can experiment with witty and clever word banter and word play with another book (and word) lover, to study and utilize mentor texts and to raise the level of their own writing. This all happens in a low-risk, less restrictive environment than what we provide through book reports or book talks or teacher-led prompt writing and other traditional reading-response methods.

The conversation journal is first and foremost a place where students are pushed and encouraged to think about and respond to literature and reading, but the reading conversation journal is also a place where students learn to carefully craft beautiful, meaningful writing, writing that moves and stirs, writing that lingers and lasts.

When Kaylee writes about her dog, Loki, "like the god of mischief," she crafts the wonderful sentence: "The name suits him." A short and powerful statement that is both playful and mischievous, just like the dog she describes.

Kaylee goes on to talk about the next book that she will read, which seemed to magically appear before her with "the sign saying in big, bold neon print 'PICK ME.'" Here she is experimenting with punctuation (commas, quotations, and ALL CAPS) while also playfully alluding to the wonderful (and strange) feeling readers sometimes experience when a book calls to them.

Finally, Kaylee ends her response with a precocious tongue-in-cheek reference to her teacher's previous response, alluding to his admission that "letting go" is a better way to think about death than "putting down." Kaylee is proud of the careful way she crafted her response ("See what I did there, Mr. Rose?") and she should be! She is learning that language can work on more than one level; she's discovering that writing can stretch meaning beyond the literal level.

Kaylee is letting go of her inhibitions associated with reading and writing.

Chapter Eight

On Reading Summaries and Retellings

As literacy educators, we have an idea of what we consider to be an "adequate" response to reading. We might even find some examples of adequate reading responses online, print them out, and then show them to the students as guides to writing or mentor texts. We use class periods to "teach" the students how to respond to a text. We give them structures in which to fit their writing. We even give them ideas to use.

Often, though, what is turned in by some students does not seem to match these "adequate" response examples that we had the students study. Not even close. What we get at first, because students are not comfortable or familiar with responding in meaningful ways to the texts that they read, are retellings. Lengthy retellings of the plot of the book. It is important, though, to remember that recalling plot and sequencing is not all bad. In fact, we have to know the plot, the sequence of events, the connectedness of the story to move on to bigger, more meaningful ideas about the text.

It is quite common for students to start with summary and retelling.

Kaylee: I am reading two books right now. But today i have my backup book Sideways Stories of Wayside School. This is a very, unique book. Everything is done wrong, the school which was suppose to be 1 stories with 30 rooms is 30 stories with 1 room on each floor. My other book Lost boy is very interesting too, it is about a boy who has moved to a new town for little bit, and is having dreams or, real life scenarios with a car, tree trunk, and his bike. When this first happens he is riding his bike when he sees a car coming and the car scares him to the side of the road where he crashes do to a tree trunk with his initials carved into them. He thinks he has died but soon realizes he' still alive. He finds his friends and stays with them to hangout when they see Wil, an old man that everyone in the town knows. His friends soon tell him that Wil killed a boy their age and got away with it. He gets home and realizes that the town has a lot of bookstores, his parents also own one. He then has the same scenario happen but this time he can't look away from the initials and he hears whispers in his ears. But wake up. He then sees Wil in their shop and can't help but want to say something to him, but before he could his mother comes in and takes control, afterwards, he and his friends all tell each other they will go to his property and sneak around.

Early in the year, teachers will see many entries like this last one from Kaylee. Big, elaborate "summaries" of their book (or backup book!). Long-winded and often full of just about every detail (major and minor) from the text, these "summaries" are not true summaries at all but rather a retelling (sometimes word for word) of the book's plot.

At first, reading and writing teachers might cringe when reading these verbose, regurgitated, low-level globs of response writing.

The real beauty and art of these conversation journals, though, is the flexibility of teaching each individual student based on the responses they provide. The student can only bring to the table the reading response skills and resources they have acquired up to this point in their schooling. If plot regurgitation is what the student wants (and needs) to write, then that is what the teacher should use to propel instruction and inquiry in subsequent entries.

So for some readers, recounting the plot of their book in great detail may be a necessary reading-response skill to practice. It is not a necessary skill for all, though, and depending on the reader, a teacher might encourage or discourage plot-recall responses.

Based on Kaylee's previous entries (and the most recent), her teacher might feel that she is ready to start pushing beyond plot recall, and so he might hit her with a series of questions designed to get her thinking about her reading outside of the book—in a more personal way.

Chapter Nine

Questions That Move Readers Forward

Getting students to think, talk, and write about reading and how it is (or could be) an intimate part of their life and growth as a student, a brother, a sister, a son, a human being, is essential. Teachers can initiate and support these radical thoughts and ideas students are having about the connection between reading and life. As teachers, we are so lucky to be a part of these powerful and potentially life-altering conversations!

Some of the best reading "lessons" that happen by way of the Reading Conversation Journal involve simply granting students the opportunity (usually through a series of pointed questions) to voice these undeniably personal connections that arise with books and reading.

Teacher: How is everything, Kaylee? I have a few questions for you: How many books have your read on your own this school year? What are you finding out about yourself as a reader this year? What are the benefits of reading for 10 minutes every day in ELA class? How are you showing growth as a reader in 8th grade?

Kaylee: this year i have read so far 7 books, I have finished 5 of them. This year I am finding out that I read slowly but am deeply into my book, and if I truly like the book I will keep reading it and I will finish it. I think the benefits of reading everyday are 1. I would never read out of class, and I don't really know why I don't 2. Being able to read for 10 minutes a day causes my brain to open more like a book, I read the pages and my brain is open to every question. And 3. I think reading everyday in 1st period helps me out a lot, example; if I read in 9th period everyday, I wouldn't have any other class to spread the knowledge to.

Teacher: This is a great way to describe the feeling one gets while reading—the mind opening up. LOVE IT! Good point! Spread the knowledge . . . love it! Interesting. Do you think you could try to find some time to read outside of class this quarter, Kaylee? I think you would start to finish A LOT more books!

Kaylee: if I read more outside of school, I think I would be more outgoing and open minded. I think I would be more outgoing because of all the adventures I would read about in all the books I would finish. I would be more open minded because of how the characters just go out and talk, me on the other hand, I keep most of my thoughts to myself, and most of the time to my friends too. I talk a lot to my friends, but if I don't trust you, you'll see me be way more quiet. So I think that reading outside of school on my own time will help me fix all of that. I just need to get some good books!

Before we delve into author's purpose and main idea and symbolic significance and intended meaning versus literal meaning, it might be prudent for readers to have a firm grasp on and understanding of their own reading process. A firm grasp and understanding of where reading "fits" into one's busy schedule and the purposes it can serve.

Most teachers are hyperaware of the idea that what they teach must be applicable to the real world. Students always want to know: *When will I ever use this?* And so teachers are forever trying to show students where it all fits: the exercise in PE, the knitting in home and careers, 3D printing in technology, poetry, algebra, World War II, and biomes . . . they all have a place inside and outside the classroom. Teachers go into great detail in elaborate monologues about how the world uses this information, these concepts; they spend weeks, months building lessons around these units of study.

But what about reading? What about good old-fashioned choice reading? Where are all the classroom objectives dedicated to choice reading and illustrating how reading fits into the world outside the classroom? Reading, it seems, is just, well . . . expected. A mandatory skill for students to possess. A prerequisite after kindergarten. But when do kids get time to read what they want to read (after elementary school)? When do teachers rekindle the reading fire and passion? When and how do teachers feed the flame?

Where are the units dedicated to building self-aware readers? Units with topic headings like: "The Art of Reading," "Finding Time for Independent Reading Outside of School," "The Art of Choosing the Right Book," "How We Read Differently in Different Genres," "The Importance of Reading for Pleasure at All Ages," "Using Reading as a Mindful Activity," "Reading Aloud vs. Reading Silently," "Varying One's Pace while Reading," "Punctuation and Reading," "Writing Meaningful Reading Response," "Using Reading to Fix a Problem or Road-Bump in Your Life" (just to name a few).

A Few Professional Texts That Help Teachers Plan Lessons and Units about Reading and Writing

Atwell, N., & Atwell Merkel, A. (2016). *The reading zone: How to help kids become skilled, passionate, habitual, critical readers.* Scholastic Inc.

Fecho, B. (2011). *Writing in the dialogical classroom: Students and teachers responding to the texts of their lives.* National Council of Teachers of English.

Gallagher, K., & Kittel, P. (2018). *180 days: Two teachers and the quest to engage and empower adolescents.* Heinemann.

Kittel, P. (2013). *Book love: Developing depth, stamina, and passion in adolescent readers.* Heinemann.

So when Kaylee figures out that she "reads slowly [but is] deeply into her book" and if she "truly likes a book [then] she will finish it," these are no small realizations. When Kaylee comes to understand that when she reads her mind "opens up like a book" and that she can "spread the knowledge [of what she reads] to other classes throughout the day," she is learning so many integral and life-related reading lessons.

The Reading Conversation Journal gives readers (and teachers) a chance to slow down, to reflect, to place their reading (and learning) process in a petri dish and then under a microscope, and what they find sometimes changes the course of their literacy lives, forever.

Teacher: So, what kind of book are you reading now? What kind of a book do you want to read next? This is a very smart way to think about reading, Kaylee. You are right. Reading opens so many doors and can change the way we view our place in the world. Let's keep working to find great books for you so that you will WANT to read outside of school, OK? This is a smart way to be. I am the same way. I do A LOT of listening before I decide to get involved in a conversation. I also feel like I want to choose my words carefully so that I don't offend anyone.

Kaylee: I'm not quiet [quite] reading any books right now, I wasn't quiet [quite] into *Brown Girl Dreaming* but I'm not finding any books I really like, I want to read one of your new books but I can't remember what it's called! It's something like deep sea or something? I don't know. It is about someone who's upset or related to that. But you didn't read it out loud so I couldn't see if I truly liked it or not. But I really need help finding a good book that suits me, I need some help. Maybe a book with relatable text? A novel with adventure, nothing that wouldn't be real. Maybe a little poetry or something like that. I don't think I'm truly into the novels in verse. I didn't like that book you recommended for me. Sorry.

Teacher: NO problem. We can keep trying!! Um, which book did you like the most this year? Which one did you not want to stop reading? I love how specific you are getting with the kind of book you like! This is showing a lot of growth, Kaylee. Keep being a 'picky' reader! That way you will never be 'bored' with a book!!! *Challenger Deep* by Neal Shusterman. I left a link to the preview. Read the preview and see if it is still something you want to read, ok?

Link to the Challenger Deep Book Preview

https://www.amazon.com/Challenger-Deep-Neal-Shusterman/dp/0061134147

FINAL THOUGHTS

How important are motivation, interest, trust, and confidence to adolescents at this time in their lives? How important are these social-emotional aspects of learning to teachers who find themselves at a loss for how to motivate, build trust, build confidence, and make connections with their young readers and writers? As evidenced in the ongoing dialogue between Kaylee and her teacher, simply providing her opportunities for free choice reading and writing guided by thoughtful prompts and responses has yielded numerous literacy benefits in just the first few months of eighth grade. The RCJ offers both teacher and students a place to explore their own unique ways of living and learning through reading and writing.

Further Reading on Affective Literacy Education

Panofsky, C., Eanet, M., & Wolpow, R. (n.d.). *Literacy and the affective domain: Three perspectives.* Retrieved August 25, 2020, from http://www.americanreadingforum. org/yearbook/yearbooks/01_yearbook/html/03_Panofsky

Part III

How Online Reading Conversation Journals Promote "Universe as Text"

Human art, whether in the form of a novel, a painting, a song, or a poem, is a pathway to truth.—Amy Casey

Chapter Ten

Expanding Our Definition of *Text*

So what happens when students don't want to talk or write about books? What do we do? How might we respond? This is a *reading* conversation journal after all—it is supposed to be a place for meaningful talk about literature. We're looking for student writing full of paragraphs, chapters, and high-level vocabulary . . . complex text, right? What should teachers write in response to student entries like these?

Leslie: So about *Pitch Perfect*, I love the songs they sing. I love hearing all of the different acapella groups competing to win. I love all of the funny things that happen in the movie.

Patrick: Something else that I think you'd be interested in is that I spent about a day with one of my mother's patients who's 102 years old. Okay, that part you may not be interested in, but here's what you would be. She has been wanting me to type up a few poems that she rewrote from her recollection of hearing them when she was a little girl. Her parents were Irish immigrants, so they were all Irish poems. I took my handy little 10 year old MacBook with me, and I typed them all up for her while she read them.

Aren't these response journals supposed to keep the dialogue keyed into topics like character development, plot structure, point of view, perspective, and author's theme and purpose? What can literacy instructors do when students choose to veer off the beaten path and engage us in topics like video games, complications at home, movies and television, Netflix, their favorite YouTuber, paintings, poems, daily obsessions, favorite hobbies, and, yes, even 102-year-old Irish neighbors?

The answer: utilize student passions and interests to fuel meaningful writing and reading. Wield what they love, and weave it into teaching by recommending books with more precision, by framing responses back to students in ways that allow them to continue to learn and write with the voice, immediacy, and intensity of someone desperate to tell their story, desperate to show what they know, desperate to grow and learn at their own pace and in a safe environment of their choosing.

Award-winning teacher-educator and veteran middle school ELA teacher Nancie Atwell (2014) tells us what she believes to be the most important factor in helping middle-level students move through this transitional stage and become more engaged in reading and writing: "allowing them agency in choosing their topics." When teachers begin to free themselves from having to make every choice of literature selection and writing topic for every student, more authentic literacy learning can happen.

In their book *Beyond Literary Analysis: Teaching Students to Write with Passion and Authority about Any Text,* Marchetti and O'Dell (2018) challenge the traditional notions of analytic writing (think dusty library reference books and five-paragraph literary essays) by inviting students to delve into their passions and pushing us to expand our view of text to include "new-age" genres such as television, movies, music, sports, and video games.

This broadening of the definition of *text* allows for the reading and exploration and analysis of much more than just books, and, the authors argue, leads to more authentic analytic writing that stands in sharp contrast to the formulaic, robotic literary essays with which English teachers have become so familiar. Marchetti and O'Dell (2018) comment:

> Something wonderful happens when we stop putting all our energy into teaching the symbolism in *Heart of Darkness* just so students can write about the theme of the novel. Instead, when we invite students to bring their individual expertise to English class, we all get to fully focus on one thing—writing instruction. (p. 27)

Amy Casey's teaching blog (www.universeastext.com) is a treasure trove of teaching ideas and ways teachers can encourage students to expand their view of text. Her argument is that nearly everything can be seen as a text because as students interact with any given text anywhere in the world around them, they can notice things about it; observe its ways of being, its features, its structures; "read" an intent, make meaning with the creator of the text; wonder about it; interpret its symbols; analyze it; compare it to other texts—the possibilities are endless.

As seen from the variety of responses that lead off this chapter, student interest and expertise can vary greatly, but the flexibility of the Reading Conversation Journal provides teachers a chance to tap into this great expanse of student know-how, allowing writing and reading instruction to happen more authentically and at a pace tailored to each individual student. But to do this, we can push the standard vision of text (and literary analysis writing) to include the ever-expanding, media-saturated universe that students inhabit.

This means the teacher sees text as more than just chapter books, nonfiction articles, and political cartoons copied in bulk and supplied by the classroom teacher. He recognizes that student worlds outside of school are dominated by Snapchat, YouTube, and the latest video game craze—advertisements and multimedia clips bombard them from the moment their eyes have the ability to sustain focus on a screen—movies, songs, poetry, ads, lists, artwork, billboards, menus, podcasts, blogs, texts, posts, posters, skits, and on and on and on.

We know that students have (or will have) access to social media from the time they wake up in the morning to the time they decide to shut their eyes at night. Information and news, both fake and real, are streaming and scrolling on student phones and laptops every minute of every day. Shows, videos, tutorials, how-to presentations, compilations, highlight reels, live broadcasts, replays, and so much more can be pulled up and viewed in seconds.

The universe is truly at students' fingertips.

With this never-ending onslaught of data, we can expand our vision of text to allow students to read and digest information in many different ways. We realize that if we want students to respond in meaningful, important ways, then we must offer them choice in selecting text that makes them want to say something meaningful and important. We do this by not only acknowledging what students are reading these days but also providing students with the types of reading material that they see and use in their own worlds.

The online RCJ provides a perfect platform to help us stay current. The teacher asks continuous questions of his readers, questions that will give him the insight he needs to teach with more precision: What are you watching on YouTube? Which media and social platforms are most fun for you to share and capture information? Which kinds of digital reading are you most interested in right now? Which Netflix or Hulu series do you love watching and talking about? What video game is dominating the XBOX scene this month?

And always: What's next? What is on the horizon? What will kids be talking about two years, five years, fifteen years from now, and how can we stay in stride? How can we keep up?

It is a daunting task, but a task integral to the further development of our literacy students. The more in tune we can be with the kinds of texts with which students are engaging and interacting, the better prepared we will be to grow their reading and writing skills through the Reading Conversation Journal.

Chapter Eleven

Tapping into Student Interests

September is an exciting (and stressful) time of year, for both teachers and incoming students. Teachers are juggling everything new: schedules, student names, IEPs and 504s, student allergy and medication lists, parent requests, seating charts, administrator and district directives and initiatives, testing schedules, assemblies, supply lists, establishing a routine, planning for instruction with team teachers, planning for school pictures.

And that's not all. We meet with special education teachers, ELL teachers, and mentors and mentees; look at test scores and district goals and objectives; set up our classroom and bulletin boards; review bell and lunch schedules; complete first-week lesson plans; attend faculty meetings; set up class rosters and grading programs; and (don't forget) get to know each and every student (and their names) who will walk through the classroom door on day 1!

The first Friday of each year, the teacher introduces the RCJ to his students and uses the first few entries to get to know students beyond their "school" persona. What follows is a typical journal inquiry from the teacher to his students in September:

Teacher: Besides talking about books, what do you spend most of your time doing outside of school? Do you have anything about which you are truly passionate? Do you have a favorite band or artist? Favorite song? What do you do with yourself when you have time off from school? What would a perfect day look like for you? Looking forward to reading your response!

This seemingly simple teacher inquiry generates a fantastic and critical variety of responses and insight into each and every one of his students. Let's face it: getting any eighth-grade student to speak out in class about *anything*, let alone their personal interests, passions, and beliefs, is difficult.

The online journal is a "safe" line of communication between teacher and student, a private space with no real strings attached: no judgment, no rubrics, no word or paragraph count, no worries about spelling, grammar, or punctuation rules—just a consistent back and forth with a teacher who wants to know more about one of his students and is interested in listening (and responding) to their thoughts on reading and writing, books, school, life, movies, sports, music, personal choices, stressors, difficulties, or anything else that comes up.

A teacher who is interested in teaching that one individual student.

This teacher is also keenly aware that he is a single, split-second blip on the middle school daily radar screen that includes eight (or more) other periods, interactions with twenty or more adults (think teachers, bus drivers, breakfast and lunchroom monitors, librarians, hall monitors, administrators), bus rides, breakfast and lunch room experiences, substitute teachers, locker room changing, swim class, hallways, stairwells, after school-study halls, and later in the day, tutoring, sports practices, music lessons, theater productions, Snapchat and Facebook posts, chores, babysitting siblings, and finally (hopefully) sleep.

The middle schooler's day is all at once amazingly stressful, incredibly fast-paced, and emotionally draining. It's no wonder they skip breakfast for that extra twenty minutes of sleep every morning! But how many adults stop to interact with each and every student every single day? Hopefully, all of them.

In looking at the whirlwind that is the elementary and middle and high school day, we understand that unless we and other adults deliberately and purposefully schedule times to interact individually with these high-speed, high-volume, high-stress students, days turn to weeks, weeks to months, and then 180 days have gone by.

And another year has passed. Another student group gone.

The Reading Conversation Journal is a place where teachers can deepen reading and writing connections with *all* of their students. A place where teacher and student can slow down, breathe, reflect, and build literacy skills at a controlled pace (set by the student) and in an environment that anticipates and utilizes student interests and passions to accelerate motivation and learning.

The RCJ is a place to deepen teacher-student connections.

Let's take a look at some student RCJ responses from early on in the school year that teach us about our students' reading interests other than traditional chap books, and responses that also illustrate the variety of passions and interests that students bring to the teaching table.

The following chapter contains RCJ exchanges (with analysis) that help illustrate how the "teaching" process unfolds when students begin to veer away from traditional texts. Notice how the teacher does not shy away from this new-age material, but instead seeks to get students thinking and learning and growing as literacy students by engaging their passions and interests and expanding his view of what constitutes a text.

Chapter Twelve

Mining Student Data

Meet Jamal, Maddie, and Natalie

How can information from Reading Conversation Journal entries help reading/writing teachers accelerate the literacy development of their students? In this section you will meet three eighth graders whose reading responses have taken this teacher in new and interesting directions. Jamal, Maddie, and Natalie are all readers, but not always in the traditional sense. They each bring a unique set of interests and passions into the classroom community that prompt us to expand our definition of *text*. Their entries are formative data that teach us how to respond next to move them further along their reading/writing continuum.

JAMAL

Jamal: There are quite a few things I enjoy doing. One thing that takes up most of my time, is during the summer and occasionally during the school year, I volunteer at Fort Ontario. I am immensely interested in history (especially military history) and being at the Fort is just one way I get to live it out myself. You may be able to catch me in a few pictures on their Facebook page. I am the 2nd youngest volunteer there. Everybody else is either 16 or up, which is quite unusual considering I am such close friends with most of the volunteers. But during the school year, I have other hobbies I enjoy. I considerably like models (boats, figures, etc. the type you put together, for example a Titanic model.) and painting them, I enjoy playing video games (most definitely not Fortnite, but especially Halo, haha), and reading. Oh, and I do enjoy eating. My mother will sometimes get angry at me for eating everything in the house. I especially enjoy eating pepperoni and crackers. And the crackers are these nice, buttery, rectangular shaped ones that just go PERFECTLY with the pepperoni. Another activity that I've recently started, is I am attempting to re-create a small section of a WW1 trench using our old garden as a frame. My goal is to make it at least 6 feet deep (I apologize, I can't remember the width of it). It's slow going, but it'll be all worth it when it's done. I plan on reinforcing the dirt walls with wood, and lining the floor with wood just like they would've back in 1914–1918. Now for music. One specific singer I enjoy listening to is Owl City, also known as Adam Young. He is most well known for his song 'Fireflies' back in the early 2000s. I strangely enough enjoy listening to some old songs mainly ranging from the 60s all the way to today. My music taste is quite diverse, and not enjoyed by many my age. I also have a soft spot for 80s music. Don't know why, I just do. I also enjoy cameras and photography. My only guess is that this interest started a few years back when I discovered stop-motion. Also I must say, I have a very, very soft and tender spot for nostalgia. I'm not exactly sure why, but the thoughts of old things I used to do, games I used to play, friends that I can't find, music, just the flow of life, how things seemed simpler, I could rant on and on. Speaking of ranting, I'll stop here, I could probably fill a page and a half just typing out my hobbies.

Wow.

Students have so many rich and rewarding passions and interests. And all the teacher had to do was ask!!

Okay, Jamal has said a lot. But his entry is fairly typical for middle-level students when given a chance to write about their passions and interests. These teens want to share; they want to write; they want to tell their story.

So many rich and exciting things happen to these students beyond the classroom walls. Their lives are overflowing with activities and lessons, interests and frustrations, loves and hates, longing and opportunity. What do we learn about Jamal through his detailed, well-written, expansive response?

So much!

What stands out most to the teacher is Jamal's love of history and the wonderful ways history weaves its way through his life outside of school. The fact that Jamal volunteers at Fort Ontario during the summer and *loves* it will be an excellent teaching tool the teacher can use to build Jamal's interest and engagement in the development and progression of his reading and writing skillset throughout the school year.

Offering book recommendations ranging from local history (Reed et al., 2000) to young adult historical fiction (Amazon, n.d.b) to war books (Amazon, n.d.c), the teacher is now in a position to provide Jamal with the kinds of texts that he will read with vigor and passion, texts that he will stay up all night reading, texts that will accelerate and challenge his knowledge of history, texts that will help him delve deeper into what he loves and cares about, texts that will surely help him hone and develop the knowledge and skills he will utilize after high school.

We might even send a short video related to Fort Ontario's historical significance (Lear, 2012) and ask Jamal to explain what is happening in the video, giving Jamal the chance to put his expertise on display (in writing, of course!). Or, the teacher could ask him to put together a short video detailing the outfit he wears when reenacting at the fort, and then share that video in his reading journal.

Through Jamal's one journal entry, his teacher has uncovered an arsenal of teaching and engagement tools. How much easier it will be to keep Jamal interested and challenged as a reader and writer! How much more quickly we can get Jamal writing and thinking in critical and analytic ways about the world. With the power of the internet at the ready, his teacher truly has the textual universe at his fingertips for Jamal—war movie trailers like *Saving Private Ryan* and *Pearl Harbor*, websites about old cameras and stop animation, music videos from the 1960s right on up through the 1980s, model plane building how-tos, and even the official live "Fireflies" video by Owl City (2016).

Rather than assign another reading with short-answer essay questions or a book report centered around finding the author's message or central idea, a five-paragraph response, or a read-this-and-write-a-summary to Jamal, his teacher is using Jamal's interests as fuel for the fire that he will create and tend to in his writing this year.

Let's imagine how this teacher could use Jamal's interests in addition to the textual universe, to open a conversation that pushes Jamal to think more critically, more analytically about how his passions and interests can become the basis for higher-level thinking practice that moves beyond the typical "read and respond with details from the text" routine followed in so many ELA classrooms.

The teacher might watch the official live video for "Fireflies" and write to Jamal:

Teacher: After watching the video for Fireflies, I am struck by the way that words and music can move a crowd. Why do you think so many people (yourself included) are drawn to this song? What about this particular music or lyrics is so appealing to us? What do you notice about the crowd that is interesting? What do you think the chorus means? What is the process that songwriter Adam Young used to write Fireflies (Young, 2019; read the article and respond!)?

Here's another way the teacher might respond to Jamal:

> Teacher: Have you ever tried to write a song? Use Fireflies as a mentor text and write me a song about some big idea you have about the world. Which protagonist from your reading this year does this song make you think of? Explain. Which line in Fireflies shows the best writing technique (according to what we have talked about in class this year)? What would a world without music be like? Can you write the beginning of a fictional narrative which helps illustrate a world with no music?

When a teacher takes the time to uncover a student's interests, an instructional universe opens up—opportunities for enhancing reading, writing, and literacy development present themselves and allow for meaningful learning and much more natural and organic growth.

This book is not discouraging response essays or teacher-directed literary response or even book reports or reviews. This teacher has utilized all of these response methods in his class (and more). But he also realized that the balance between teacher-directed, tightly structured, on-demand response writing and free and open textual response writing was off, had shifted so that most of the writing he was doing in his classroom was of the tightly formulaic kind. Necessary? Yes. But he wanted to offer students more of a balance between the two types of writing. The RCJ helps address this writing balance issue in his classroom.

Teachers can get students reading and writing with more immediacy, more verve, more vigor. Teachers can reawaken in students that sleeping love of words and books, sentences and stories, rhythm and rhyme, but they must be willing and ready to move beyond chapter books and nonfiction articles (when necessary) to get kids talking.

The first step in building readers and writers who care is always asking them: *What do you love?*

MADDIE

Maddie: The things that I really enjoy doing are; playing lacrosse, soccer, and hockey. I also love to play golf and swim in the summertime. I also like playing viola. I am actually going out to Boston today, for a lacrosse tournament, and Cleveland for hockey next weekend. My favorite band is the Decemberists, my favorite song is Once in My Life, by the Decemberists, Beginning Song, and Make You Better, all by that band. Another thing I am passionate about is juggling, I have been trying to perfect my behind the back and under the leg move, I can start with both but can't quite do them while I'm juggling. A perfect day for me would be to wake up around 7 or 8, get right up, take my dog Phoebe on a walk. Then I would want to eat pancakes for breakfast. Then, I would go swimming, and to end it off eat dinner at Rudy's. My favorite show is Gossip Girl and I like to watch it on Netflix.

Though Maddie's response is concise, it is packed full of information that will help her teacher not only connect with her and deepen the teacher/student relationship, but also allow her interests to play a part in the development of her reading and writing persona. Whenever he feels that Maddie is lacking in motivation or struggling to find something to read or reaching a learning plateau, he can go back to this entry and mine it again to help propel Maddie forward, sustain her interest, and give her the boost she needs to move forward with her literacy development.

Let's take a closer look at how Maddie's interests could help accelerate her literacy growth.

The fact that Maddie is traveling to different cities and states on the weekend to play different sports is significant and tells her teacher a lot about her. Maddie's weekends are not "relaxing"—she does not have much down time. Saturdays and Sundays for Maddie seem tightly scheduled and full of long car or bus rides, locker-room chatter, and competitive, high-level physical activity. Maddie, it seems, arrives home late Sunday nights after strenuous activity, only to get up early Monday morning for school.

The fact that her grades have been exceptional in the years leading up to eighth grade (according to her online folder), and that she is a top-notch student (in all her classes) despite her heavy extracurricular schedule outside of school, tells us not only that she can handle the load but also that she excels in this type of environment, that Maddie thrives when challenged to do more, say more, think more deeply.

Her teacher is already anticipating what Maddie might read this year and putting together a list of possible books tailored to her lifestyle—classics that will prepare her for honors English next year (*Catcher in the Rye*, *The Old Man and the Sea*, *To Kill a Mockingbird*), motivational books by and about female business leaders (*Road to Power: How GMs Mary Barra Shattered the Glass Ceiling* or *Becoming* by Michelle Obama), self-help books about staying organized and engaged with a busy schedule (*The Productivity Project: Accomplishing More by Managing Your Time, Attention, and Energy* by Chris Bailey), and motivational sports books like *A Team of Their Own: How an International Sisterhood Made Olympic History* by Seth Berkman (2019).

Looking deeper into Maddie's entry, the teacher notes that the Decemberists are her favorite band. After a quick Google search, he finds out that the Decemberists are an Indie Rock back from Portland, Oregon, with quite a following. They are a five-person band who came together in 2000 and have been playing ever since. Colin Meloy (lead singer, guitar) is the principal songwriter.

The teacher goes on to listen to and watch the Decemberists' ("The De-cemberists," 2020) official video for "Make Me Better" (The Decemberists, 2014) on VEVO.

The song and video are great, and the teacher wonders why he has never heard of this band before. The band has put out eight albums to date and has had one song ("Down by the Water"; thomyorke74, n.d.) nominated for a Grammy Award.

But the key to all of this it that takes time to learn about Maddie's favorite band, takes time to listen to a song or two, takes time to look at images of the band, to read about them. He understands that taking time to learn more about each of his students will make him a better teacher, will give him chances to push Maddie to grow and develop her literacy skills in much more engaging and meaningful ways than the typical "read this article and re-spond" or "write a report on the book that we read in class" assignment.

The teacher could copy and paste the chorus from a Decemberist song ("Here I Dreamt I Was an Architect"[1]) and see if Maddie can make connec-tions between the lyrics and the book she is currently reading (*The Catcher in the Rye* by J. D. Salinger):

> And I am nothing of a builder
> But here I dream I was an architect
> And I built this balustrade
> To keep you home, to keep you safe
> From the outside world
> But the angles and the corners
> Even though my work is unparalleled
> They never seemed to meet
> This structure fell about our feet
> And we were free to go

Or the opening verse to one of her "favorite" songs, "Once in My Life"[2] :

> For once in my life I have someone who needs me
> Someone I've needed so long
> For once unafraid I can go where life leads me
> Somehow I know I'll be strong

Using lyrics from Maddie's favorite songs to get her thinking more deep-ly about the books that she reads and the characters with whom she is inter-acting will ensure that she is motivated and challenged to think in new and different ways about those texts. This process will also keep Maddie on track with the development of her literacy skills. Maddie would be comparing, contrasting, evaluating, looking for similarities and differences between the two texts, analyzing, and formulating a sort of thesis or argument to show how the texts connect (or not).

What will she say about how Holden Caulfield's characteristics, hopes, dreams, actions, and desires overlap with the Decemberists' lyrics? How do the themes in *The Catcher in the Rye* and the song "Once in My Life" overlap or intersect? The learning process becomes more meaningful and powerful for Maddie when her interests are taken into account.

NATALIE

Natalie: I absolutely love dance so so much. I have done dance since I was five (2010), but I did skip a year in (2013) I don't even know why. Most of my friends are from dance and I get to see them at school all day everyday, and then I see them at dance for endless hours. I don't know what I would do without dance. I love being able to tell a story through movement. I know a lot of people who have an argument, if dance is or isn't a sport. I both agree and disagree. I play sports and I also do dance. I know that there is huge differences in some aspects but is very similar in others. I know that we warm-up similar (conditioning wise), but dance has a bit more stretching. Other things could be like some compete, some have games, but how do you really classify something as a sport?

Let's take a close look at this new and exciting response from Natalie.

The excerpt from her Reading Conversation Journal reveals a deep passion for dance. When Natalie comments that she "does not know what she would do without dance" and that she "love(s) being able to tell a story through movement," her teacher takes note and realizes that for this particular student, dance could be utilized to build rapport and literacy learning opportunities throughout the year.

Her teacher sees that Natalie might be interested in debating the argument that dance is not a sport. He might offer her an article like "Dance Is Not a Sport: Here's Why It's So Much More" (Linnihan, 2016)," giving her an opportunity to read the article and respond with her own argument for her favorite pastime.

He could also begin to recommend books related to Natalie's love for dance. He might provide her with a list of fiction books (Amazon, n.d.a), or he could generate a link to a list of nonfiction books (Barnes & Noble, n.d.).

The online Reading Conversation Journal is a wonderful place to offer book recommendations, allowing students to browse the lists at their leisure and at their own pace. It's a way for us to use student passions and interests to zero in on book lists and individual book recommendations quickly. Giving students the chance to choose their own texts to read while also providing students with books that overlap interests, passions, and pastimes ensures that students will be reading, writing, thinking and sharing with more immediacy and a sense of urgency and engagement that will get them writing more, and more often.

Her teacher could also get Natalie thinking about her future, and how dance could be a part of that future. It is never too soon to get students thinking about life after high school, after graduation. Planting seeds early and often will give students a chance to start to prime long-term goals, to start thinking about career choices, to start seeing the connections between the passions and interests they have now and the jobs and careers available to people with those interests and passions.

The reading journal can become a place where these initial discussions and conversations can take place, where teacher and student project forward and dream about what lies ahead.

The Reading Conversation Journal can help students visualize their future.

Her teacher might ask Natalie questions like: *What aspect of dance do you like most?* Or *Where do you see yourself with regard to dance in ten or twenty years?* Or *Do you know which colleges offer dance majors?* Or *Besides being a professional dancer, do you know of any careers that involve dance and by which people make money? Who is your favorite dancer?*

If Natalie shows interest in her responses to these more specific questions about dance, her teacher will guide the conversation in the appropriate direction. If she seems turned off by these questions, if she doesn't seem to want to engage in a conversation about her future at this time, he can shift the discussion in a different direction.

But always, this teacher is willing and ready to use the "universe" to guide literacy instruction. Dance videos, dance blogs (Energetiks, n.d.), dance TV shows (*Dance Moms*), dance movies (*Step Up*), dance magazines, and dance vlogs—the possibilities for texts that will push Natalie to write and grow as a literacy student (and stay engaged in the process) are endless.

The universe is hers for the taking.

NOTES

1. Reprint permission granted by Laura Bergstein, Redlight Management, December 10, 2019.

2. Reprint permission granted by Sarah Pilotte, Sync Licensing Coordinator, Songtrust, March 23, 2020.

Chapter Thirteen

The Universe of Digital Media

YouTube, TV, Movies

It is clear that to get students writing in meaningful ways about text, a teacher should first understand and engage a student's passions and interests and then expand their own view of what constitutes a text. The online Reading Conversation Journal presents the perfect opportunity to uncover students' interests and start to use them as a means of accelerated literacy growth.

So, what sorts of written material are worthy of attention these days?

Beyond chapter books, newspaper articles, and textbooks, what are today's students spending time reading, watching, and studying outside of school? As already seen, asking students early on in the year to share their passions and interests gives the teacher a chance to start to understand who each student truly is—the kinds of things that make them tick, the stuff in which they are emotionally invested.

The stuff that gets their hearts pumping.

When someone is doing something that they love to do, their emotions and level of focus are heightened; their awareness of their surroundings becomes exponentially greater; their memory and stamina increase; their ability to reason and formulate ideas and opinions grows along with their ability to analyze, synthesize, evaluate, and comprehend.

To see this in action, all one has to do is watch and listen to teens viewing YouTube. They sit, pupils glued to screen, back straight, phone or remote or tablet or laptop in hand, half smile painted on their faces, eyes wide, attention tuned to the action on the screen. They giggle, laugh, guffaw, gasp, pop their hand over their mouth, grow teary-eyed, share and send messages, save, and manipulate. They scroll. They search.

But mostly they watch . . . watch . . . watch.

For hours and hours on end they watch. They observe. And they would continue watching if not forced to get off, to go outside, to watch something on "normal TV."

Educators and parents could easily play the role of police, condemning YouTube and Netflix, glossing it over, marginalizing it, even demonizing it by saying things like "It's making kids inactive and unhealthy" or "It's causing kids to be lazy" or "The stuff they watch on YouTube is trash with no content. Useless. A waste of time." Teachers could continue to warn students about the hazards of too much screen time, too little face-to-face interaction, too little conversation and outdoor activity, without offering viable alternatives. "Nobody talks to anyone anymore!"

Or, teachers can find out what students like to watch for hours on end and use that information to accelerate and reinvigorate students' will to write in meaningful and important ways. Writing and reading teachers can allow YouTube, television, and movies to be the "text" that spurs their readers to write, the text that guides their students into thinking more deeply about life and the world around them, pushes them to practice the kind of writing they will use in college and career and life.

Listen to eighth grader Sadie talk about her favorite YouTuber:

Sadie: I love Joey Graceffa's YouTube videos. He's a great person...Yes, I'll link a couple of Joey's videos. Joey has a gaming channel and a vlogging channel. He plays a lot of minecraft, he's been taking products and mixing them together lately, like all types of chocolate. I think he's popular for the sheer fact that he's a great person. He's funny, he loves animals, he's passionate about certain things etc. I did know he wrote a book but just never got around to reading it . . . yes, I really love that Joey is famous because he is himself, and I love that he shares a lot with his subscribers. I feel like in this generation it's so easy to become a famous person in someway. I feel like since people are always on YouTube and looking for something to watch because they're bored, it's easy for someone to stumble upon a person's channel, love them, and subscribe. I think YouTube is good and bad in some cases. People like to escape from the real world, and people get bored. But I feel like it's bad because people who like to say rude things about other people to make themselves feel better, do it a lot on YouTube.

It is clear that Sadie is answering questions posed in the previous entry by her teacher. Here, she begins to formulate an opinion or idea that might become the basis for an essay about the push and pull of YouTube, the agony and the ecstasy of the digital video platform, the goods and the bads associated with being a teenager who recognizes that social media outlets allow for freedom of expression but also freedom to bad-mouth and bully.

We can use Sadie's interest in YouTube (and a very specific YouTuber) to help her begin to formulate ideas about how the world in which she lives works, how decisions are made, how people behave, and what she can do (or not do) to make the world a better place.

The safe environment created by the teacher within the conversation journal becomes a place where Sadie can begin to articulate her complex ideas about the texts with which she is interacting and accelerate her thinking. Her teacher will continue to prod and poke, stir and whisk, pry and inquire so that Sadie's ideas gradually become more complex and more articulate.

Netflix and other streaming television services can also become a textual platform through which complex and high-level thought and discussion can occur. Listen to Tom talk excitedly about his favorite show *Stranger Things*:

Tom: Yes I have seen *Stranger Things*!! I LOVE IT!!!!! My favorite series by far. I love the teenage drama that's weaved in with this sci-fi story. I like how mike and El have this unbreakable bond. The last episode was my favorite when they were at the snowball dance, but I felt bad for Steve, because Nancy left him for Johnathan Buyers. I wanted the creators to give a little more of a back story on the "Shadow Monster" . . . But I like how it keeps you in suspense. I love how Dustin had a great friendship with a demogorgan.

After watching the final episode of *Stranger Things* for himself (okay, maybe he binge-watched the entire collection of episodes from the very first one), his teacher would be well prepared to respond to Tom. A resourceful teacher might send Tom a review of the final episode and ask him what he thinks about the author's take (Kain, 2019) and how Tom's own views connect or disconnect with these ideas.

It is clear through Tom's entry that he is most interested in the relationships established, broken, maintained, or developed between and among characters. Can his teacher get Tom to expand and extrapolate out his thoughts and feelings around these complex character relationships? Of course he can.

Now that his teacher knows that this show gets Tom's heart pumping, as long as he asks the right questions, Tom will engage in conversation. Tom would not be nearly as spirited or as interesting or as motivated if he were required to read and respond to, say, chapter 4 of a historical fiction novel assigned by the teacher to the entire class for homework. Just asking questions like: *How does Dustin show that he is friends with the demogorgan?* Or *What do you know about the shadowmonster and why do you think the writers are not providing much of a backstory for this particular character?* Or *How has Mike and El's relationship changed over the course of the season?* Or *What examples of teenage drama is going on in season 3 and what do these parts do for the story?* should be enough to get Tom writing and pushing himself to think about his text in new and critical ways.

Depending on what he already knows about the learner, this teacher might ramp up or ramp down the number and complexity of his questions in his response. If the reader/writer has a history of being reluctant, struggles with writing fluency, and has had a hard time elaborating on prior responses, the teacher will lighten the load, providing one or two specific, straightforward questions about *Stranger Things,* or possibly using one of Gallagher and Kittle's (2018) favorite conferencing lines, "What about this text is worth talking about?"

If the student has already shown that they are an avid reader and fluent writer with the ability to analyze text at a high level, the teacher would be more apt to ramp up his response, offering comparisons to other texts, supplying supplemental questions and material for further reading or investigation, urging the reader to explore other avenues of thought and reasoning or even research.

The learner leads the conversation.

Read again how Leslie excitedly talks about and leads a conversation about her favorite movie series:

Leslie: So about *Pitch Perfect,* I love the songs they sing. I love hearing all of the different acapella groups competing to win. I love all of the funny things that happen in the movie. Plus if you like the first one there is *Pitch Perfect 2-3* also. When I watch all of them I like the songs equally. The third one is great and funny but when I went to see it in the theater it was not what I thought it would be about. In each of the movies there is a big event that effects the movie.

But that event is always hilarious.

I hope you and your family like these movies as much as I like these movies.

So In the first movie it starts off with the old Barden Bellas (The main acapella group) and something happens (watch and see!). So this event forces the Barden Bellas not to proceed to the finals. So all of the old Bellas graduate except for two, Chloe and Aubrey. So they have auditions and there isn't a very good "selection". Then this one girl, Becca is late to the audition. So she sings "The Cup Song". Many new girls make the group, including Becca. So Aubrey really wants to win because of the "event" that happens the previous year.(you'll see why!!!!!!).

So every year the Bellas do the same routine and it has gotten them pretty far. Aubrey is the leader of the Bellas so she decides to do the same routine. Well Becca (very into mash-ups and modern songs) sees that in their first performance, everyone was going on their phones and not listening to the performance and the judges were shaking their heads.

When the teacher asks eighth graders to provide a list of their favorite books and authors at the start of the school year, many cannot provide a single book or author, but when he asks about their favorite movies, the lists are extensive. Why not engage these cinema fanatics in a bit of critical thinking and writing through the guise of the big screen? When he found that Leslie was writing journal responses that lacked elaboration and voice, he asked her about her favorite movie and received the above entry in response.

It is easy to see that when Leslie begins to write about the *Pitch Perfect* movie series, directed by Jason Moore and starring Anna Kendrick, her attention is heightened, her voice is more evident, and she elaborates, paying particular attention to the plot of the movie, the action, the high point, the suspense, the critical moments and ideas. She summarizes the movie without giving the whole thing away ("you'll see why!!").

Using movies as a text to which students can respond opens a whole new world of possible conversations ranging from movies turned books (or vice versa) to discussions about directorial and writer decisions regarding the plot structure, to specific actor and actress performances, to movie reviews and online review sites like Rotten Tomatoes, to the differences and similarities between reading and watching a movie.

So much to see, so much to talk about.

So many directions we could go. Her teacher will (of course) watch *Pitch Perfect* now that Leslie has enticed him with her descriptions, but before he does he asks Leslie if the film would be suitable for his family—specifically his six-year-old daughter Ellie, to which Leslie responds:

> I don't think you should watch *Pitch Perfect* with young kids. I watched it when I was 10 and it has some pretty inappropriate things in it. I watch the movies over again and I think to myself "Did it say that the first time???" And yes it did. It also has a little bit of swearing.

Her teacher could choose to ask Leslie about the movie rating system, ask her to do a little research about how movies are given a rating, the process associated with it. Maybe he asks Leslie to make a list of ten movies that she would recommend for his family and why the movies would be good for the make-up of viewers in his family. The possibilities are endless.

But it all comes about as a result of the student leading the way. The learner. Who are they, and what do they like?

The universe is out there, waiting to be explored.

Chapter Fourteen

The Video Game Universe

Meet Ricky and Sebastian

In the summer of 2019, in a sold-out arena in Shanghai, China, the International DOTA 2 Championships gave away over 34 million dollars in prize money to the winning teams at the event. According to Dexerto.com, almost 2 million fans watched the video game tournament, including over 1 million viewers on Twitch, the live-streaming video platform by which gamers watch each other play (think ESPN for Esports).

At the time of this writing, Epic Games' mega-popular battle royal game Fortnite has over 250 million registered players, and the number is growing at a rapid pace. Esports (professional, multiplayer video-game competitions) is now a multi-billion-dollar worldwide industry, and most school-age children are right in the middle of it all. Listen to these eighth-grade gamers talk passionately about their favorite pastime:

Terry: I actually play video games from like 3pm to 10pm, now I do take a couple breaks for dinner and family, and weekends, I can't even say, I am literally on the entire day and into the night or I am at my friends houses. But sometimes my parents make me spend time with the family so it isnt that number straight, but for me I play until I go to sleep basically, so that can be almost 12 hours on a weekend I don't have to do anything unless I have to do chores or go somewhere, you probably get the point by now.

Ricky: Okay so I'm gonna tell you straight up! I am not much of a reader at all. But that doesn't mean the books are bad. I like a few of them even some that I love because their classics. But the reason I don't read much is that I have a ton of video games at home and I mean a LOT OF THEM!! So I tend to enjoy that experience because you don't have to think you just play and enjoy the ride along with your skills and techniques.

Most educators have seen the incredible impact of gaming on young lives (especially young male lives) firsthand, and this teacher has been watching his own son Sebastian (age 13 as of 2020) grow up with, play, talk about, read about, debate, observe, study, socialize, compete against, struggle to learn, and research, research, *research* video games, ever since his tiny hands could manipulate a controller.

Sebastian has read articles and reviews on games he wants to buy with his chore money, watched hours and hours of streaming video on gaming technique and highlight packages, studied how-to videos about setting up a controller for maximum player speed and efficiency, researched the start-up cost of an at-home gaming studio complete with bidirectional polar pattern mic to capture audio from front to back, noise-cancelling headsets, and a quality gaming laptop (among other things).

Playing video games is how Sebastian relaxes after school, passes time during holidays, socializes with his friends, tests his gaming ability in a competitive environment, and builds lasting friendships. Gaming is how Sebastian (and many other middle school students) establish and grow relationships and status in today's world. For students like Ricky and Terry (above), gaming is what gives them life and pushes them to be better people.

Gaming is the lifeblood of many of our students.

Thus, video games offer the teacher another text avenue to explore and analyze in the Reading Conversation Journal.

After the teacher found himself struggling to get much writing from Ricky in his RCJ, he tried a different avenue based on Ricky's self-proclaimed "obsession" with video games. When he revealed to Ricky that he was trying to decide if he should buy the hugely popular first-person shooter video game Call of Duty (COD; published by Activision) for his then-ten-year-old son, Ricky's writing took on new life, new energy, especially when he began to argue against another popular video game called Grand Theft Auto (GTA):

Ricky: But the game you should NEVER AND I MEAN NEVER give to a child is this horrific game series called GTA aka Grand Theft Auto, even the name is bad! Here's what this game has in it: Drugs, alcohol, prostitutes, swearing, nudity, racial offence, shooting INNOCENT PEOPLE AND COPS! And many more bad things! MY MOM DOESN'T CARE IF I PLAY ANY OTHER GAME BESIDES THAT ONE SHE BANNED ME FROM EVER PLAYING THAT GAME UNTIL I AM 20

YEARS OLD!!!!! And the sad thing is, is that my younger cousin Jackson WHICH IS IN 3RD GRADE PLAYS THAT GAME AND HE NOW KNOWS EVERYTHING THAT THERE IS IN THAT GAME AND HE IS NOT A GOOD KID BECAUSE OF IT!!!!! Tell your son this when he is 13 years old you will get for his birthday and ONLY play it for 2 hours a day so he doesn't always have that killing stuff in his head which makes him think its ok, I swear ask him that and it's a win win situation but with GTA wait until he's like 18 or 19 and still set a time limit for like 3 hours of GTA when he's that age ALSO before I forget, let him know that Call of Duty can ONLY be played in his room with the door shut so his younger sibling don't see it!

Ricky's previous journal entries (in response to "traditional" text) had been robotic, one- or two-sentence retellings of the plot of his book. Lifeless and dull, Ricky's responses lacked passion and authenticity. When his teacher takes time to get to know Ricky's passions and interests, expresses an interest in them, and then allows his vision of text to stretch beyond the traditional novel, a different universe opens up, a new and exciting (and familiar) platform for Ricky to practice the art of response writing—a place full of opportunity and self-discovery. A frontier full of opportunities for exploration and experimentation and growth.

Ricky's above response is an exercise in argument and persuasion where he is ultimately joining the discussion on the age-appropriateness of video games, the difficulties of setting screen-time limits, and the complexity families have with multiple kids at multiple ages playing video games under the same roof. His teacher can think of many new and exciting writing and reading avenues they can now explore together.

His teacher might send Ricky an article or two about the effects of hours of daily screen time on teens or the possible impacts of violent video games or an opinion piece about the negative or positive effects of video games on teens' lives or an infographic that shows that the average "gamer" spends close to a thousand dollars a year on video games or a top 10 list of tips and tricks to play COD better or a particularly scathing video review of COD.

Once again, a universe of reading and writing possibilities opens up. Instead of inundating Ricky with pages and pages of irrelevant text and information, the teacher decides to keep the discussion centered around his own son, and more specifically that he is truly wrestling with the idea that his son is infatuated with a war game:

Teacher: BTW . . . my son is trying to convince me that he is mature enough to handle Call of Duty Black Ops. He has been trying to persuade me for about a year now and there is just one hurdle that I can't seem to clear in my mind. I can't make myself understand how war could be a game, ya know? Like, I can't see my other 2 kids walking by the TV while my son is slitting some guy's throat with a knife and thinking that is ok or fun somehow. I know you probably have some thoughts on this so I will put it out there for you to respond to. He is in 6th grade - about to be 12 years of age. A good kid, never gets in trouble. Smart. I just can't get over the fact that Call of Duty is a war 'GAME.' War is not a game. We should not treat it like it is.

This teacher takes advantage of the unique time in his life when he is experiencing something so relevant, so near and dear to the hearts of his students. He is allowing himself to be vulnerable and open, to let his guard down in hopes that it will spur his students to see and understand that literacy—specifically information-gathering and reading and writing—can and should play a significant role in people's lives.

His teacher is also not afraid to expose Ricky to a series of complex ideas, ones that the teacher himself has been struggling with as his own child grows older, and the idea that war would be considered a game, that war is something kids play. When the teacher takes a chance and writes in honest, complex, vulnerable ways, he is rewarded with meaningful written responses from his students, writing that is authentic and purposeful in that it offers chances for his students to think deeply about the texts with which they are currently engaged:

Ricky: And with killing someone thats not supposed to be fun or ok but then again it's war so you kinda have to survive or YOUR dead or buy the game now and have the same rules applied and that should help, your welcome! Ok after all I heard from your response I know what you should do next if he can understand the death and scarness of someone dying then honestly have him only play once a day so it feels like he died like an actually soldier BUT their is something else also, there's a lot of mean people on there that swear and make racist comments because I've been in that situation myself when I played Call of Duty but I only play because my friends play it, but instead of that game I will suggest some games like Fortnite which is survival, Battlefield which is a better version of Call of Duty which is also a war game plus no one else really has a mic to swear and make racist comments, Kingdoms and Castles and Kingdom and its sequel Kingdom: New Lands which are building games and survival with battles with dragons and vikings most of all I think he will like Battlefield more than Call of Duty.

There is much to "teach" in regard to this response. The entry is somewhat difficult to read due to a lack of punctuation and spacing. This is a lesson that the teacher can and should provide, and now he can provide the lesson in context, showing Ricky how he can better control the reading pace with punctuation, how spacing and paragraphing can help the reader better process what he is saying and help group the big ideas Ricky wants to express. A lesson taking small chunks of Ricky's response and revising them with proper punctuation and spacing might go a long way for future entries.

Showing Ricky how a small section of his own writing can improve with punctuation and spacing will go a lot further than a revision worksheet or even a peer-editing workshop. Here his teacher takes the time to show Ricky an edited version of Ricky's entry:

Ricky's Entry: And with killing someone thats not supposed to be fun or ok but then again it's war so you kinda have to survive or YOUR dead or buy the game now and have the same rules applied and that should help, your welcome!

The teacher's edited version: And with killing someone . . . that's not supposed to be fun or OK! Then again, it's WAR so you kinda HAVE to survive or YOU'RE dead. Buy the game now, and have the same rules apply, and that should help. YOU'RE WELCOME!!!!

These more "formal" writing lessons become a bit tricky, however. The teacher does not want to stunt Ricky's creativity and willingness to write and elaborate on his own complex thinking. Although it is easy for writing teachers to want to start to "fix" and correct Ricky's work, we must weigh the consequences carefully.

Sometimes, good teachers realize that we must make certain sacrifices for the greater good of the writer. We realize that learning to write in more sophisticated, meaningful ways is a slow process and varies from individual to individual. We must know each one of our students well in order to make the important decisions associated with moving middle-level readers and writers along the literacy-development continuum.

What is a more important skill to be taught at this point in Ricky's progression as a writer? Is it more important that he learn the proper way to use apostrophes in contractions, or is it more important for Ricky to begin to express his complex thoughts and views on text in more than just a few drab sentences?

Chapter Fifteen

The Universe of Poetry and Song

Meet Owen

Poetry, song lyrics, and books in verse can open up a brand-new universe of reading response for teacher and students.

Why poetry and songs? As Roy Peter Clark (2014) resounds in his brief but beautiful book *How to Write Short*, "There may be no more efficient form of short writing than the song lyric." And this efficiency that Clark speaks of is what draws many students into the world of poetry and into the universe of the song.

Authors of Young Adult literature have taken note of this attraction students have to poetry due to its efficiency or, more specifically, the limited number of words on a page, the amount of white space, and the speed with which a page of poetry can be read in comparison to a page of prose. In a time when people make a living off of 140-character tweets, and the most at-home "reading" being done by students are the 150–200 text messages they get to before bed, it's nice to know that poetry and lyrics are there to be read and studied and analyzed with the same ferocity and attention that we pay to a good Hemingway or Joyce narrative.

This teacher offers poetry, songs, and books in verse to all students, but particularly to students who are struggling with reading stamina. Here, *reading stamina* is defined as the ability of a reader to read with focus and understanding for consecutive minutes without stopping or taking a break.

The teacher will specifically offer books in verse to students who start and stop books often, students who complain that books always "get boring" after the first thirty pages or so, and students who admit that they have not read a complete novel in the past three or four years (or ever). Books in verse offer readers a chance to grow their confidence, a chance to experience a whole book, sometimes for the first time, start to finish.

The lyric offers students a quickly readable, complex text without the high number of words per page that often discourages certain readers from even starting a book, let alone actually reading the first few chapters.

The versatility of poetry is also worth noting. Words written in verse can be read (and enjoyed) for surface meaning, literal meaning including sound, rhythm, and rhyme. But poetry, as teachers know, can be read at a second, deeper level as well. Poetry can push readers to explore the idea of metaphor and allusion, the idea of multiple or layered meanings. A poem, too, does not have to be fully understood to be appreciated; maybe a certain line, or word, just resonates with a reader.

In the case of the song lyric, readers are offered even more to "analyze" and think about in the way of the music (and usually the music video) that accompanies the words, added layers of meaning and interpretation that can help a reader understand the poem or lyric on a whole new level, thus gaining a deeper appreciation for the text. The amount of extra work that middle-level readers will put into their favorite songs and music videos in an attempt to uncover more meaning is at once staggering and inspiring.

Owen liked to read books. He was an avid reader who responded in his online Reading Conversation Journal every week, wrote about the books he was reading with a brief summary, a synopsis of the plot up to that point in the story, a brief update of the characters, a small commentary on the quality of the text, and a salutation to his teacher, offering him a "good day" and a "see you next week!"

The responses were all fine. But was Owen being pushed to explore the texts that he was reading in deeper, more complex, more meaningful ways? Was Owen being given a chance to share his expertise about a particular area of interest with his teacher? Was Owen being given a chance to explore how the texts he loved and returned to often inform the way he interacts with the world? Was Owen being given a chance to push his reader-response skills beyond "here's a summary of the book I read because the teacher said I had to"?

His teacher knew that Owen had more in him. He knew that Owen could produce deeper, more meaningful thinking if steered in the right direction. Where did he look for inspiration? Owen's September entry, of course, which deftly and completely outlined in perfect detail Owen's love of rock music. What if his teacher pushed beyond Owen's chapter-book reading? What if he delved deeper into Owen's love of music?

Once he knew Owen "better," the teacher steered the conversation toward music, admitting to Owen that he loved rock music, particularly classic rock like the Doors, Led Zeppelin, and a punk rock, garage-sounding band who grew to popularity in the 1990s (when his teacher graduated high school!)

called Weezer. Owen's response opened the door to deeper, more meaningful conversation about literature:

> Owen: If you like rock music, I got a band for you. Check out the band Otherwise. Search the song I don't apologize. That song inspires me because I want to be a songwriter and singer. Adrian Patrick (who I know and am friends with, I met him at the Oswego Boxing Club), sings with such emotion. The lyrics also strike me right at the heart.

Now we're on to something! Owen is starting to open up, to share his story. It is clear, even from Owen's response, that his passion for rock music runs deeper than just listening to the occasional ACDC record; Owen not only names a song that "inspires" him but also follows a local band, knows the frontman, and wants to be a songwriter and singer himself!

This is the kind of entry that excites us, gets us fired up about the RCJ and teaching. When teachers can strike a nerve in their writing students, when reading teachers can find the pulse of the reader, then they become the ultimate, true master teacher, someone in a position to not only motivate their students to read and write better but also guide and inspire them to continue on a path toward their destiny—their life's work.

With passions "in hand," the Reading Conversation Journal becomes much more than just a place for practicing reading response; the conversation journal becomes a therapeutic, restorative, mindful meditation in how to utilize literature and worldly texts as motivation to mold and move students along a learning continuum that will ultimately lead them down their path of dreams and aspirations.

The conversations in this RCJ help students start to visualize the connections between what they are reading and how that connects with where their lives are headed.

Once his teacher opens up about his love of rock music, Owen continues to say more about his deep love of music. Listen as Owen talks (eloquently) about one of his favorite songs, "Zombie" (a remake) by Bad Wolves:

> Owen: Have you heard the cover of Zombie. The original was by The Cranberries, but Bad Wolves made a cover. The original was good, but Tommy's vocals took it one step higher. I like the music video of the Bad Wolves version. It includes a woman that is painted gold and dressed like an egyptian. She starts rubbing the paint onto a glass wall separating the band from her. She first draws the numbers, 1-15-18. I noticed a couple of things about this music video. For one, The egyptian style costume. In the music video by the Cranberries, the lead singer Dolores O'Riordan, is dressed up in this exact costume. This is a great nod to the original. Another is the painting. I believe it is to symbolize the bridge between

Dolores and the world being sealed away. A final thing I noticed is those numbers. 1-15-18 is an important date to this song. January 15th, 2018, was the day that Dolores O'Riordan died. Bad Wolves put this cover out to support her family, not for profit, so it makes since that they would add this important date.

Original: https://www.youtube.com/watch?v=6Ejga4kJUts

Bad Wolves: https://www.youtube.com/watch?v=9XaS93WMRQQ

Oh, and I'm going to see Bad Wolves live sometime this summer. They are touring with Five Finger Death Punch.

Where to start with this entry?!

Ultimately, the teacher is mining for gold at the start of each year. Each student, each reader, offers a chance to strike it rich.

With Owen, the teacher has struck gold.

To have a reader digging deeper into a text, truly exploring the text, opening it up for further discovery in a way that is both organic and enriching . . . it is the "rush" that reading teachers are after day in and day out.

What makes teachers do what they do, minute after minute, day after day, week after week, even when some days the water is rough and murky and the thought of finding anything (let alone a gold nugget) is overwhelming and so far out of reach?

It's the knowing that there is a chance to strike it rich.

In this beautifully constructed entry, Owen is using his love of music, along with one of his favorite bands and songs, in conjunction with two music videos, to analyze, compare and contrast, and begin to ultimately construct theories about lyrics and the poetry of Dolores O'Riordan, the former lead singer of the Irish rock group the Cranberries, whose haunting lyrics to "Zombie" still linger in his teacher's ears to this day.

Your minds might be going a mile a minute at this point. How should his teacher respond to Owen?

Let's explore some of the possibilities a teacher could indulge in the journal with Owen at this particular point in his learning progression. It is important to remember that these possibilities only come about as a result of the environment created by the journal, an environment of recurring, low-stress, encouraging, inquisitive talk centered around texts chosen by the student.

Anytime a student leaves a link, the teacher finds himself clicking and viewing first. He, like many of his students, can't help but follow links. Links are like a sugary treat, or a crunchy, salty potato chip—one link leads to another, which in turn leads to another, and then it is four hours later and the bag is empty, the sun is down, and the battery to the computer is dead (the only thing that pulls the eyes away from the screen).

The exchange of links is also essential to these journals.

Offering links to students (thus opening up the internet world) is a key advantage of the online journal. Book lists from Barnes and Noble and Goodreads, articles and interviews with authors, trailers for movie versions of the books students read, music videos, book trailers, Amazon previews, cover shots, reviews, public library catalogs, history and science videos—so many engaging, enriching ways to help readers grow and develop. The internet is a treasure chest of seemingly unlimited riches for the middle-school reader. Any reader really.

Teacher to student or student to teacher, links promote more engaging, enriching discussions and connections in a more sophisticated learning environment.

Owen's links help showcase the original "Zombie" (by the Cranberries) to the remake (by the Bad Wolves), which leads quite naturally to the comparison of not only the two music videos but also to the subtle changes in the lyrics of the two singers and the melodic differences in the tone of the two versions.

After viewing the original music video of "Zombie" (the Cranberries), his teacher is struck by the religious and political imagery portrayed in the visual images. He notices a crown of thorns, a cross, soldiers, and guns—the song is ripe for interpretation and offers literally hundreds of pathways to analysis, deeper thought and insight and practice in developing complex ideas and sustaining literary theories and claims.

But this teacher always allows the student to choose the path of the conversation, to move and build ideas on their own, to propel themselves forward at a pace and intensity set by them, for them. It is important that the teacher not monopolize the conversation at this point.

It would be easy for the teacher to allow his love of interpretation and literary analysis to sort of take over and thus push Owen into the background, leaving him in the dust as the "expert" begins to offer his deep thoughts on the religious allegory running through the song and video and how the zombie, for more than eighty years, has been a symbol used by filmmakers as a metaphor to represent the deeper, darker fears of Americans including political unrest and overthrow, or how "Zombie" was written by O'Riordan after a bomb planted by Irish republicans went off in Warrington city center, killing two kids, age 12 and 3, and injuring dozens more.

How "Zombie" is a battle cry, an ode to end war and the thoughtless violence that accompanies it.

The teacher needs to try, for the most part, to keep his views and ideas separate for the moment, and accentuate and help Owen tease out, elaborate on, and further define his own.

In his RCJ entry, Owen has shown interest and curiosity in certain areas of the song and the video for "Zombie," including (but not limited to):

1. the difference in the vocals of the two singers;
2. the Egyptian motif that runs through the video;
3. the differences and similarities between the two videos;
4. the symbolism of the glass and the gold painting in the Bad Wolves music video of the song;
5. the importance of the date written on the window; and
6. the way one videos alludes to the other (Owen makes mention of how one band "nods" to the other).

So much to talk about, such rich and meaningful directions and paths Owen and his teacher can travel! The groundwork for high-level discussion has been laid, and Owen is the conductor, leading the conversation at a comfortable pace and depth.

His teacher could ask Owen questions to help him further elaborate on one of his ideas: "Can you tell me more about the Egyptian costume worn in the videos?" Or "What other sorts of symbolic representation do you notice in the music videos and what might they indicate or represent?" Or "What is one of the main differences you notice between the 2 music videos?" Or "How do the Bad Wolves change the lyrics of *Zombie* from the original version? Why do you think they do this?"

He could also get Owen to start thinking about the challenges associated with remaking a song that was already so popular. What type of song makes for a good remake? Why does a group want to remake a song? What makes a song remarkable? If you had to pick an older song to remake, what would it be and why?

Simple questions on the surface, the teacher uses these inquiries to get the reader thinking and then responding, saying more about something that they noticed in a text. He could also bring Owen back to the book that he is reading, ask Owen to compare the themes and ideas in "Zombie" with the themes and ideas in the book that he is reading, get him looking for overlap, get him thinking about writers or how many themes and messages are universal.

What about the lyrics to the song "Zombie"? Can't the teacher take the first verse to the song and allow Owen the chance to analyze? Yes! So many possibilities abound.

The teacher will push Owen to keep talking about music and the texts that already inhabit his life, the texts for which he is already so interested, the reading material he picks and chooses of his own accord and on a daily basis.

Further along in their discussion, Owen begins to discuss another of his favorite bands, Nothing More, and more specifically their song "Jenny." Owen shares his expertise of the band and the song:

> Owen: I like sharing music to others, and trying to show people new things. There is another couple songs that you may like that are on their namesake album. They are "Jenny," "This is The Time," and "Here's to The Heartache." One interesting, but sad thing, about the song Jenny is that it is written about the singer's sister. When she was born, she had the umbilical cord wrapped around her neck, and was lacking oxygen. Her mother always new something was wrong with her after that. After that, her mother had gotten cancer. She started with drugs after that. When her mom died, she went crazy.

It is worth noting here that Owen, like any eighth grader, loves sharing his knowledge, loves having someone to talk to, loves building and maintaining a trusting relationship with another human being. But mostly, Owen loves being able to communicate what he loves in a nonjudgmental environment with someone who he knows will respect his opinions and push him to delve deeper, push him to read the texts he loves with greater attention and care, and with a wider, more worldly focus.

This is motivation, confidence, trust, self-awareness, and engagement all wrapped up into one teacher-student relationship created by talking through reading and writing.

In the above example, the teacher finds another rich RCJ entry, full of chances to teach and ideas that can help Owen develop his literacy skills. When Owen says that he likes "sharing music to others and trying to show people new things," it is an invitation, a learning well that his teacher can tap for a fruitful, more exciting year of skill-building and literary discussion.

Owen begins to talk about the song "Jenny," connecting the story behind the song with the lyrics, building interpretation of those lyrics through the lens of his prior knowledge about the lead singer's life and the band's historical context. Just as teachers and students would take into account the time period associated with when a story or poem was written, Owen has naturally, organically shifted the RCJ discussion to a place of deep inquiry and complex thought.

Owen first recounts Jonny Hawkins's tragic life, the difficulties associated with the birth of his sister, and the frontman's mother's subsequent demise and fall from grace, her seeming inability to "heal" from the difficult birth of her daughter and the health problems that arose as a result of the complicated delivery of the baby. Owen is utilizing this prior knowledge to inform his interpretation of the lyrics to the song, and he is doing it, for the most part, without a teacher's persuasion, without a bulleted, multi-tiered essay question tied to an elaborate analytic rubric. Owen is using a text he loves and cares about to inform his discussion and thought.

In which directions could a reading teacher tug Owen so that he begins to build his analytic skills?

A teacher might focus on expanding Owen's interpretation of one particular stanza, allowing Owen to work on his elaboration skills, his stringing together of first sentences, and next paragraphs, all connected to a complicated idea grounded in a common text (in this case one stanza of one of his favorite songs). The teacher might ask Owen questions like: *How does the first stanza help reveal the idea that Jenny is lacking oxygen? Which lines and words help to create an atmosphere of need? What is the visual the author creates in this first stanza that would help support your theory about Jenny and the umbilical cord issue during birth?*

Maybe Owen can use this song as a mentor text and write a song of his own that contains many of the same elements of "Jenny." Maybe Owen can write a memoir that captures a difficult moment from his own life. Maybe Owen would like to explore the songwriting process, research Nothing More, and study the writing process of Jonny Hawkins and the other band members. Would Owen like to read some reviews of his favorite band's most recent shows? Could Owen write his own reviews of Nothing More's songs, concerts, and albums?

Yes.

It's all right in front of him. In front of them.

The teacher need only continue the conversation.

Chapter Sixteen

The Universe of Art

Meet Jacinta

It was clear from the beginning of the year that Jacinta wanted to talk about much more than just books. A quiet student who never spoke up in class (even when called upon to speak), Jacinta would try her best to blend in with the background, the classroom walls. She was the kind of student who would be perfectly fine going through the year not saying anything, never raising her hand, never offering her ideas or opinions.

Clearly, after reading just a little bit of Jacinta's writing, we see she has a lot to say. How many students struggle to speak up in class, to express themselves, to voice their complex ideas and deeper thoughts? How many middle-level students are nervous to reveal their "true" voice in front of other students for fear of looking stupid or too smart or getting it wrong or being laughed at? Her teacher knows that these feelings of doubt experienced in the classroom are often unfounded, but he also knows that the conversation journal is a space where students can explore this inner, more complicated voice without fear of retribution or retaliation from other students.

Jacinta would do fine in this teacher's class; that was clear from what her teacher observed on the first day of school. Jacinta was organized, did everything that was asked of her, expressed herself well through writing, and was adept at using the English language. Jacinta would get an A in this class (and all her other classes for that matter) probably without ever really having to offer up any complex ideas or sustained deep thinking.

Listen as she describes her thoughts on responding to traditional text:

Jacinta: I do things differently than other people as I read and this (writing about what we read) just doesn't appeal to my way of reading. I also have

85

a higher level of reading than most. . . . But I think I've definitely improved in my reading habits . . . you kind of harped on us about reading
which I actually am thankful for because I've gotten in touch with reading
again. Still, my only goal for reading and writing this year is to make
more time for it. But I still do enjoy the analyzing stuff that you give for
me. And that's where I feel like the reading conversation journal has been
helping me. Writing about my book and my reading, it just doesn't appeal
to me. . . . By the way, can you give me more things to analyze? Like
anything. Quotes, poems, pictures, songs, videos, maybe even movies or
something. I love to analyze things and I enjoyed analyzing that picture
you gave me. I guess I'm a pretty analytical thinker. I've always loved
puzzles and those brain teaser type things and riddles too. And that's
funny because I have pretty much no common sense.

The RCJ is a place where a teacher can spark and support sustained mental
meditations and complex written thoughts and ideas with nontraditional
texts. Jacinta is begging to explore texts outside the norm.

If a student does all of her work, takes good notes in class, hands everything in on time, completes tasks outside of school, and is not a behavior
problem, she will most likely do well in school, even without engaging in
classroom discussions. Not to mention how incredibly difficult it is for teachers with large classes to engage every student's provocative thoughts and
ideas.

After all, there is curriculum to teach, standards to uphold, tests and
quizzes to offer, homework to assign and grade, labs to deliver, vocabulary
instruction, district initiatives to consider, daily classroom goals and objectives to visit and revisit, data to collect and analyze, and administrators to
report to—the world of a teacher is so much more than just a well-thought-
out lesson plan. Teachers welcome those students like Jacinta, students who
do everything that they ask, and do it well.

The RCJ offers Jacinta a weekly chance to elaborate on and explore some
of those more sophisticated thoughts she is having about the texts with which
she is coming into contact. It provides Jacinta a chance to speak out, to shout
if she wants to!

When her teacher recognized that Jacinta was sort of "going through the
motions" with her RCJ entries—that is, responding to the books she was
reading by basically summarizing the pages she had read—he offered her a
piece of digital artwork to analyze, hoping to get more out of her conversation journal thoughts and ideas. Here is the image and what Jacinta said about
it (Tangoself 12/7/13, zhidao.baidu.com):

Jacinta: I think I do agree with the picture because reading takes you to
new heights, new places and new worlds. Sometimes reading can be an

adventure and you can learn so much. Let's say the light blue/flowery/ butterfly area is our world. Our reality. Someone who doesn't read only knows that. Just like that one dude who isn't standing on any books. The middle guy is standing on a few books but just enough to see the "next level" (the world of reading). The person seems to not be in the "next level" yet. So this may represent people who read a good amount but not in depth enough. It's pretty dark in the beginning because it's only just the beginning or it represents the challenge of not wanting to read. They can see the benefits of reading but maybe haven't experience it just quite yet. But the last dude, the ones who is standing on a lot of books, he has risen above all the darkness and sees a beautiful sunset. This represents people who love reading and read a lot. They know the benefits of reading. And the've experienced it too. They've maybe gotten past all the challenges that may come with reading. Because they read in such a way. Reading has taken them to new heights and they can see, in this case, a beautiful sunset.

Wow. Jacinta has given her teacher so much more than just the drab summary! Here is a student who never says a word in class opening up through her writing, first offering analysis of a complex text and then supporting that analysis with exact references and details from that text.

Visual images bombard students these days, from short advertisements before and after YouTube videos and "free" music accounts, to flashing banners and scrolling product information on websites and online game sites. The daily visual assault offered through social media sites and platforms is continuous and unrelenting. It is a text with which students are very familiar.

No wonder Jacinta is so comfortable and willing to expend mental energy and thought on analyzing one image. It's an extension of the world in which she lives. Could her teacher have gone through the whole school year reading Jacinta's book summaries? Yes. And being able to summarize *is* important; it is a much-needed skill that students must work on and get better at. But in Jacinta, her teacher saw something more. She offered so much more in the way of deeper analysis and thought through artwork and digital images. Listen to a later response from Jacinta's RCJ when her teacher asks for her interpretation of a famous Edvard Munch painting called *Separation*, urging Jacinta to come up with a title for the image:

Jacinta: As for the painting, this one is very confusing. Because I've seen so many references to the different paths thing. Like choosing the path by the ocean is related to this or choosing the path through the forest means this. So this is completely my own view and I'm pretty sure I'm "wrong" but this is just how I see it. I would title this painting Decisions, Choices or Paths because, going back to the path thing I said before, I feel like the golden women person is walking on the right path so this may mean she has made good choices in life that have lead her on this path. The other dude is not on the path anymore. He looks sad and hurt judging by his facial expressions and his body language. And because he is not on the path anymore, maybe he has made some decisions in his life that have lead to him not on the right path. So I feel like the painting is telling us that our our "path", will be based on our decisions in life. I didn't really fully understand this painting as well because certain elements were confusing.

So many paths (no pun intended!) for teacher and student to tread on. So many directions in which they could travel. It's great, too, to see Jacinta use phrases like "this one is very confusing," "I'm pretty sure I'm wrong," and "I didn't really fully understand this painting," because these phrases indicate that the painting and consequent interpretation are challenging Jacinta, forcing her to push herself to think and analyze at a higher level than she is used to. After her teacher teases out Jacinta's analysis of the Munch painting, he sends her a link to a professional analysis/review of the painting, an analysis that challenges her own ideas and helps her see a differing perspective. Here is her response after reading the professional review:

Jacinta: WHOA! I never would have expected that to be the actual meaning of the painting! I do agree with that interpretation. I feel like it's a little better than mine because it talks about even more little details and meanings behind them that I would have never noticed or figured out, like the crimson plant and how it blocks the guy's path. My view on that painting was completely different! . . . The only paintings I really know are the most famous ones. Like the *Mona Lisa* and *The Starry Night*. And that's only because they are super famous.

This short but powerful exchange illustrates the flexibility of the conversation journal: its power to engage and develop the analytic skills of a reader, and the relative ease with which a teacher can tap the "universe" for nontraditional texts. Remember, too, that this is a student who rarely says anything in class, and what she does say is said with great reserve, a tiny voice, and only if "forced" by the teacher.

The conversation between teacher and student continued in the next few entries, her teacher allowing Jacinta to lead the way. After conducting some quick research on Edvard Munch paintings and the history of the painter, Jacinta challenges her teacher to interpret one of the painter's most recognizable works, *The Scream*:

Jacinta: *The Scream* by Edvard Munch. The same person who made *Separation* (I didn't notice it was by the same guy as the other one until I looked it up. I just pulled up random paintings) You interpret it because why not? It's something new and it makes you work a little. :D

What an incredibly interesting and fruitful way to practice text interpretation and critical thinking! Not to mention Jacinta's utilization of research skills to find other Munch paintings. When Jacinta asks her teacher to do some interpretation, she turns the tables, and the student has become the teacher!

One of the biggest areas of concern for this teacher as he took to the classroom in his first few years of teaching was challenging the top-tier readers and writers. The reading and reading-response lessons he taught in his first ten years of English instruction were age appropriate and fit most learners in his classroom, but it was evident that the majority of the lessons he taught were not challenging enough for the most proficient readers sitting in his classroom. They never complained, they sat quietly, they did the work asked of them, they read, they wrote, and they scored well on tests and quizzes.

Day after day, week after week, year after year, there always seemed to be four or five students per class who needed so much more than the one-size-fits-all, canned reading and reading-response lessons.

And what about the students who were reading below grade level? It was also easy to see that the lessons were too difficult for these students. These readers were easy to spot, too, often disengaging or acting out during the more direct reading/writing instruction portion of the lesson by putting their heads down on the desk or pulling out work from other classes or turning around during instruction to talk to the students behind them.

This teacher's lessons, it seemed, were successfully reaching and impacting about half of the class. Those in the middle. So what could he do about those who needed a bit less and those who needed more?

This question kept him up at night. What could he offer these students at both ends of the learning spectrum? The Reading Conversation Journal was born from this challenging classroom dilemma, this challenge of meeting the needs of all students in the reading classroom.

Her teacher then decides that Jacinta is ready to do even more challenging response writing. He gives her the famous Frost poem "The Road Not Taken" (1916), asking Jacinta to read the poem and then compare the poem and the Munch painting *Separation*. Do the ideas presented in the poem fit the painting in any way? If so, how? Why? The following excerpt from Jacinta's RCJ uses content vocabulary, appropriate transitions between ideas, higher-level compare/contrast thinking, and deep, meaningful thoughts and ideas that center around both authors' intent to portray a message to the reader:

Jacinta: I think the poem does fit the painting. First off, the poem is talking about how the traveler was kind of disappointed in not being able to take both paths and explore both. This could relate to real life because someone could be disappointed in the decision they made and maybe wondered if choosing the other decision could have led to something bigger. But I think in the end the traveler chose the path that was least traveled and it says "And that has made all the difference". This could mean that by not choosing the decision/way that most people choose, it made a big difference because they was unique and "saw" or experienced things that most people would not get the chance. This could also be a lesson or the lesson that the author of this poem was trying to convey. Also I feel like when the say "traveler" they mean people because really were all just traveling through life. I honestly don't know very much poetry. Poetry is not a topic I like. There's only a few poems I know of actually like *The Red Wheelbarrow* and *The Bells* by Edgar Allan Poe.

Could the teacher have had this rich and meaningful discussion with Jacinta "outside" of this reading journal? Probably not.

FINAL THOUGHTS

Teaching students with such a wide range of interests, abilities, prior knowledge, and experiences is challenging. We need all the help we can get in order to meet students where they are and invite them on this journey called school. The online RCJ is one way that a teacher can open up the kind of meaningful dialogue that challenges all readers and writers in personally engaging ways.

Expanding our definition of what constitutes *text* literally exposes limitless possibilities for the classroom teacher. When we bring in and honor the texts our students already love—the texts that are everywhere and highly accessible in the world they inhabit—we send the message that we care, that we are invested in their literacy learning, that we are ready and willing to learn about what matters to them, that we know that everyone learns and expresses what they know in a multitude of ways, and that we are ready to learn from them.

Everyone benefits.

Part IV

How Online Reading Conversation Journals Grow Reading Engagement and Self-Awareness

Welcome to the attention economy, in which the new scarcest resource isn't ideas or even talent, but attention itself.—Davenport and Beck (2014), cited in Hall et al., 2015

Chapter Seventeen

The Importance of Reading Engagement

Meet Lydia

In part II we learned that Kaylee is a typical student in that she came to eighth grade with the idea that her teacher would be offering only whole-class book experiences. That the entire class would only be reading and analyzing books together, slowly, carefully. "What books are we reading this year?" is a common question from English Language Arts students in September.

In middle school and in many elementary classrooms, too, reading seems to be more about teacher-selected books, usually one per quarter, with lots of "strings" attached: chapter worksheets, short- and long-response essays, vocabulary sheets, presentations, section tests, and quizzes. This general reading pattern appears to follow students through high school (and sometimes college) as well. It's no surprise, then, that Kaylee has this expectation when she arrives in eighth grade.

In part IV we learn about and from Lydia, a student whose self-awareness and thinking about her own reading preferences and processes grow in notable ways. You may notice that in the commentary segments of this chapter, we've maintained the part II themes of motivation, confidence, and trust and threaded them through these new themes of engagement and self-awareness.

We have found in our analysis of thousands of online conversations with middle-level writers that, though these specific themes are dominant in many student-teacher conversations, there are other discoveries at work as well. Our intention is to incorporate and build on the themes from previous chapters as we introduce new ideas and different young writers to you in upcoming chapters.

We believe in many pathways to literacy growth and development, the first of which is "hooking" a student on reading. Getting young readers to buy in to the powerful idea that reading books (and other texts) is a "forever" skill that enables all people to entertain themselves, to teach themselves, to push themselves outside their comfort zone, to recognize new perspectives, to fill in knowledge gaps, to empathize with the plights of others, and to make the world a better, more meaningful place in which to live. The idea is that students begin to see reading as a way to better themselves and the world around them, as well as a source of entertainment and joy.

As literacy educators, we can reinforce these values and benefits. Teachers who need to justify to themselves and others why they are "just reading" in the classroom need only look as far as the Next Generation ELA Standards (NYSED, 2017), which, in our home state of New York, have taken the place of Common Core Standards and support the value of pleasure reading in all classrooms in all content areas. We encourage teachers to also browse and share with their administrators and colleagues the National Council of Teachers of English's (2019) statement on independent reading at https://ncte.org/statement/independent-reading.

But before students recognize all that reading can do, they need motivation. They have to feel an overwhelming need to pick up a book, a desire to read. They need to feel the call of the book.

True, it might come as a bit of a shock when teachers alert their classes in September by saying something like: "Welcome students. I have great news. You will be selecting your own books to read this school year. You will read as many books as you can in the next ten months, and I will promote your reading by giving you ten minutes of independent reading time at the start of every single class period this year. Therefore, you must have a book picked out and on your desk every single day of this year, even today on the first day of school!"

It's no wonder that most eighth graders look a bit puzzled and even stressed at first. "But I don't even know what kind of books I like!" they will say. "Where do I begin?"

And so the lessons start there as we create a mindset centered around books and reading goals. Teachers might ask questions like: "What kinds of books are out there in the world and which ones suit you?" "Where can you find the books you want to read?" Similar to a librarian's "reading advisory," reading teachers can establish themselves as knowledgeable recommenders of books for individual students, setting them on their own reading path, hopefully for life.

ELA teacher Jennifer Serravallo (2017) offers teachers specific ways we can promote engagement while reading:

Being engaged means keeping not just your eyes but also your mind on the book. As you read, be aware of your attention shifting. When it does, back up and read. If you notice attention shifting very often, consider whether the book isn't a good fit or something in your environment is causing you to become distracted. (p. 25)

Article about Setting Independent Reading Goals with Students

Serravallo, J. (2017, May). Dropping everything to read? How about picking some things up? *Voices from the Middle, 24*(4), 24–27.

Conversations about the meaning of "independent reading" and what it looks like to be an engaged reader help propel readers forward. Teachers might flash a picture up of a middle school student casually propped up on a rug, leaning against a bookcase immersed in a book (Walsh & Rose, 2017). Sometimes it's necessary for teachers to explicitly reveal to their students what healthy reading behaviors look like, feel like, and what the benefits are in school and in life.

Decades of educators have relied on Louise Rosenblatt's (1994) reader-response theory, which states that what readers bring to the reading process is as much a factor in that experience as the text itself—that the reading process is, in fact, a transaction among the reader, the text, and the writer. It's about relationship.

Ivey and Johnston (2013) studied seventy adolescents in an engagement-focused eighth-grade ELA classroom in which the teacher decided to allow her students full choice when it came to reading selections, with no subsequent required assessments. Ivey's (2014) "The Social Side of Engaged Reading for Young Adolescents" teaches us: "whereas the goals of engaged reading, from an instructional perspective, are typically about getting better at reading, students who were engaged as readers viewed reading as fundamentally about working on relationships, both with others and with themselves" (p. 165).

Students attributed their social, intellectual, moral, and emotional development that year to their reading. It transformed them in unexpected ways. The researchers were most impressed by these results, especially given that the students were responsible for what they read as well as what they did with their reading. Their study opens up a multitude of conversations about the value of whole-class reads, high-stakes summative reading assessments, diagnostic reading interventions, and direct instruction in every ELA skill students need to demonstrate to perform on such interventions and assessments.

Lydia is a student who admits to not having read a single book on her own for over two years. Not that she doesn't like to read or fails to see the value in reading—it is clear that she enjoys reading when she has the right book. Lydia might be overlooked in some classrooms: she is quiet, reserved, and unwilling to raise her hand during class discussions. She walks into the room silently and exits the room silently. In a forty-three-minute class, it can be difficult to find time to connect with a student like Lydia. The Reading Conversation Journal can bring out the best in many of these students who want to hide their way through school.

> Lydia: So far this year I'm really liking independent reading a lot more. I found a book I really am enjoying! [*The Perks of Being a Wallflower*] I have also already finished a book. [*Drama*] that was a really good book. I found "The Perks Of Being A Wallflower" from you! So thank you for that. What you should know about me as a reader is I'm not interested in a bunch of books. I'm more interested in realistic fiction. I don't really like fantasy books because I'm not into all that magic type of stuff. But I'm really loving the book I'm reading now and I'm really excited to finish it.

> Teacher: So glad that you are loving reading this year, Lydia! Keep it up! Think of how many books you will have finished (and talked about) by the end of this year! Looking forward to hearing what you have to say. See if you can start to notice what makes a book good, OK? Like, what does the writer do that makes people want to keep reading the story?

A booktalk a day might be a welcome addition to any classroom routine—a one- to three-minute discussion of a high-interest text and then the subsequent reading of an excerpt from that text. If students like the sound of the book, they write the title and author down in their notebooks on their "Books to Read" list (or something similar). In Gallagher and Kittle's (2018) *180 Days*, both teachers suggest daily booktalks to capture the interest of middle-level readers. "At the beginning of the year, booktalks are critical because they generate interest in reading and help students make plans for reading" (p. 28).

We see from Lydia's initial thoughts that even though she is a quiet student who does not participate by raising her hand or offering her opinion or engaging in "out-loud talk" in the classroom, she is listening to the booktalks and participating in writing down titles in her notebook. She is also utilizing the RCJ to be more mindful about her reading experience.

The fact that she is noticing what she prefers, one genre (realistic fiction) over another (fantasy), is important if she is to get the most out of her reading this year. Lydia confesses that she is "excited to finish" her book, another sign that she is becoming hooked on reading, starting to see it as more than just a school-related activity (one often followed by chapter and vocabulary quizzes). She is becoming more aware of her reading likes and dislikes, her reading habits. She is starting to want to read.

Chapter Eighteen

Mindful Teaching, Mindful Reading

Reading is, in essence, a mindful activity. Early on, many students may struggle to read for even two or three minutes straight, often getting up out of their seat to use a tissue, get a drink, go to the lavatory. In September, readers might start nodding off a few minutes in, eyes droopy. To read well, one must set aside outside worries, outside sounds, outside distractions. To read well, one must focus in, relax internally, quiet the mind, slow the breathing, suspend stress, live in the moment, and be open to engaging with a text and that text's author.

Study: "The Power of Deep Reading and Mindful Literacy: An Innovative Approach in Contemporary Education"

Abstract: This paper explores mindfulness as an innovation for improving literacy skills of deep reading. More specifically, this paper describes a case study of a deep reading intervention where graduate education students participated in an eight-week deep reading training. As an embodied practice, deep reading serves to awaken and evoke the reader's voice, helping the learner to make meaning as a whole person immersed in the embodied nature of language. Deep reading, as other contemplative practices, requires persons to go inside, to find meaning, to know themselves, and to connect to others (Barbezat & Bush, 2014). Unlike many other contemporary approaches in education, deep reading draws upon the involvement of the whole body and mind. Deep reading provides a conduit for stretching the human capacity for imaginative thought, shows promise for developing cognition, quiets the chaos of a distracted society, and, overall, serves to humanize the educational process. (Hall et al., 2015)

How do we decide which books to talk about in class? It is a complicated answer that depends on a variety of factors, such as the time of year, the teacher's familiarity with the book, the book availability, the length of the book, the book's readability and overall appeal, the book's ability to overlap with the writing curriculum as well as other core subject areas, the book's diversity and cultural appeal, and connections to school and districtwide reading and literacy goals and targets.

The decision of what to read requires that teachers be thoughtful about the titles they choose to share in the classroom on a regular basis, books that will maximize time, impact, and engagement for students. By implementing on-going conversations, teachers can enter the minds and hearts of their students.

In September and October, teachers might choose to talk about books with wide appeal—books with 150 pages or fewer. Books with fewer words per page. Books that are relatable to the majority of students. Early on, teachers can promote books that require less reading stamina. As the reading year begins, it is all about starting and finishing books (though students are allowed to abandon books that are not working for them in favor of a new one—it's a balancing act).

Through years of conversation with eighth graders and through student survey data, we learn that middle school readers often start books but don't finish them. An instructor need only observe students independently reading for the first few weeks of school before noticing the revolving door effect, that is, the merry-go-round of books that are in and out of students' hands. Many middle-level readers will at first exchange books daily, unable to stick with a book for more than a few chapters, unable to commit to one book.

When asked about this constant swapping out, students say that they have become "bored" with the book, that they are just not "into the book" anymore. Early on in the year, students lack the ability to push through books, especially if the going gets tough, if the action dies down. Teachers can combat this lack of reading stamina by choosing to talk up books with fewer words per page, shorter chapters, more pictures and illustrations, more action. Thinner books that move.

There is power in finishing a book. It is one thing to read a book, but it is quite another to finish the book. Getting to that last page, that final line, that final word! Closing the book upon completion, that feeling of accomplishment.

Finishing a book is a feeling we want all our readers to experience early and often. This feeling propels readers to read more often and with more urgency, and so at the beginning of the school year we can promote books that provide this opportunity and experience. The feeling of turning the final page. Of closing the book for the last time. That feeling of satisfaction, or perhaps even disappointment. Readers can, however, abandon books for a variety of reasons, and that option needs to be acknowledged and offered if this is to truly be a self-selected reading experience.

Whether or not a reader stays with a book depends on many factors. Having a growing awareness of our own interests, habits, preferences, and tendencies as readers will help us set both short- and long-range goals. Through Reading Conversation Journals, literacy educators can assist readers in developing greater self-awareness and agency about these decisions.

Lydia is already hooked—it is clear in her comments. Yet this is a student who has a history of not reading, a student who has been in hiding—not because she wanted to hide, but because she may have never had an opportunity to share her thoughts and feelings for one reason or another (bigger classes, louder students, jam-packed curriculum, short periods, and district-wide literacy goals and objectives that constrain both teacher and student, to name a few).

Lydia is becoming more aware of her reading identity, and she is being spurred on by a teacher who is showing genuine interest in her as a reader (and a person). Her teacher lets Lydia know that he is happy for her while also getting her to think down the road a bit, at the possibilities of her reading future. Allowing students opportunities to consider their short- and long-term reading goals is another important objective of these early conversations.

Lydia: Thank you for the book suggestions because I'm starting to read at home more often so I'm going through "Perks of Being a Wallflower" faster than I thought! I'm a pretty slow reader and I think thats why I'm not good at reading big books because it takes me forever to finish it. But I'm trying to get there! I feel like "What Girls Are Made Of" seems interesting. Does the library have it? The librarian is borrowing "The Barrows" for me.

Teacher: Look at you, Lydia! Loving what you are reading, and being ready for what you will read next is SOOOO important. Great job getting books lined up. Did you finish 'Perks' yet, or are you still working on it? How do you like having at least 10 minutes of independent reading time in class EVERY DAY this year, Lydia? Do you think it is helping you as a reader? As a student? How many books do you think you will finish on your own this year, knowing that you will have that much reading time in class every day?

Here we can see that Lydia is growing more and more mindful of her reading habits and tendencies and recognizing how they are changing. Her own noticing that she is reading "at home more often," that she is "a slow reader," and that she is thinking about her next book is a great sign. This is the development teachers are hoping to see early on with their readers.

Teachers should expect to see readers reading, for sure, but it is important for teachers to hear readers becoming more aware, more able to articulate the inner workings of their reading development and progression toward self-selected goals.

Early on in the conversation process, teachers should also be mindful of conversations that reveal a reader becoming more confident with regard to genre choice and book selection. Teachers should expect to hear from readers like Lydia who are writing about how happy they are with their book choice and who are excited to read outside of class. Students might describe the places they like to read and their optimal reading conditions.

Ultimately, we want readers who are showing interest in finding books in new and different ways (through the public library or with the help of the librarian or through interlibrary loan). In her blogpost "How to Stop Killing the Love of Reading," Jennifer Gonzalez (2017) interviews seventh-grade ELA teacher Pernille Ripp, who calls this "book shopping." Ripp keeps a classroom library of several thousand books because she believes no two readers are alike. She wants every one of her students to find something interesting and attractive "staring them in the face" when they go book shopping. "I need to make sure that every child has a chance of finding a book that will speak to them" (Ripp in Gonzalez, 2017).

Lydia is also becoming aware of her reading resilience. She says that even though she feels like she is taking forever to read her book, she is "trying to get there." Reading resilience and stamina are two integral skills and dispositions that are difficult to teach. Her teacher thinks about stamina as the capacity to read longer, more complex texts for greater lengths of time in one sitting. He defines *reading resilience* as the ability to keep coming back again and again to a text even when we are distracted by the stimulation around us while reading: the multitude of feelings, thoughts, sounds, sensations, interruptions, plot changes, slow moments, and so on.

We can learn to become aware of and practice noticing these distractions, then intentionally return to the place we left off—and begin our reading again. It's easier to read when the action is intense and the suspense is forcing us to read on, but what happens when the action and dialogue in the book die down and the suspense retreats to the shadows? Do we quit reading? Start another book? Give up?

Unfortunately, the answer to these questions for most eighth graders at the beginning of the school year is *yes*. What do you do as a reader when the going gets tough?

Reading can be a cognitively sophisticated task in that it not only involves academic skills but also requires the conscious development of habits, attitudes, expression of emotions, dispositions, and the self-awareness of all that is happening to us and for us when we read. Mature readers and writers use their executive functioning skills regularly throughout the process of reading and writing about what they are reading.

The idea of resilience deserves more thought. How many fiction books start with an action-packed scene, deliberately grabbing the reader's attention, before promptly delving for pages and pages into backstory and exposition? How many great stories start slowly? How many of the best tales we have ever read only truly reveal themselves after the final page?

While not all books are meant to be read from start to finish, and readers ultimately choose whether or not to stick with a book, many can be so much more meaningful if we do finish them. Good readers abandon books all the time; however, in some instances, especially with fiction, the messages the book's author wants to impart, the deeper meaning and life lessons lying in wait for the reader, often come to fruition upon the book's completion.

Readers need to learn to recognize and be comfortable with ambiguity, trusting that the author will clear up confusion later, or that there is a rationale behind the confusion. We cannot allow students to miss opportunities to learn, to grow, to prosper through the reading of a book. How, then, can literacy teachers encourage this reading resilience?

Good literacy teachers rely on and explicitly and deliberately model desirable reading behaviors and attitudes. What better way to teach reading resilience than by having the teacher struggle through a book and think aloud about those struggles? Sometime in September, Lydia's teacher reveals to his students that he is attempting for the eighteenth time to read *Moby Dick*. "Seventeen different times!" he confesses to each of his classes. "Seventeen different times throughout the course of my life I have started to read this American classic, only to give up . . . quit." He holds his most recent copy of the Melville classic up for all to see.

Good literacy teachers articulate their struggles with a text: the falling asleep after half a page, the checking of the book out from the local library only to return it on the due date without ever having read a single page. Sometimes we might even lie to a group of English teachers, telling them that we have in fact recently finished the book and "Loved all 138 chapters!" Later, when one of the teachers asked about the ending the book, we might excuse ourselves to the restroom and never come back to the conversation! Are we really that much different from our students?

"But why do you continue to read a book that you obviously don't like?" students will ask with their faces all screwed up in wonder.

It is a great question. A question that teachers cannot answer all at once. A question that teachers can systematically address over the coming months on their quest to finally complete a book that has eluded them (like a white whale) up to this point in their life. A book like *Moby Dick*. A book that is giving this teacher the chance to explain the idea of reading resilience, the idea that when a book gets tough, when the reading gets rugged, a reader reads in different ways to help with focus, attention, and word recognition.

The mini-lesson options here are limitless. We can teach about reading challenging books slower and with greater care, how we must take more breaks, how we often have to read sections aloud to gain a better understanding, how we must reread often in order to clarify information and check our understanding of the text.

As teachers struggle through a text like *Moby Dick*, they can seize the opportunity to articulate the thoughts and feelings associated with reading resilience, mixing these ideas into student RCJs, knowing that students will mimic the content-specific vocabulary and language while adopting reading habits and cues.

It is possible for each of us to become so much more than just the English teacher standing in the front of the room. Through our very public struggles with challenging works like *Moby Dick*, we become real readers, just like everyone else—readers with similar thoughts and feelings about books and reading's frustrations and complications. A mindful reader takes time and care to recognize not just what we are reading but also *how* we are reading. When students recognize that their teacher has some of the same thoughts and feelings about reading that they do, it is a powerful moment.

So when Lydia says that she is "trying to get there," she is hinting at resilience, a skill she is seeing modeled every day by a teacher silently reading *Moby Dick* at the front of the room (most of the time with a perplexed look on his face).

Chapter Nineteen

Teaching the Whole Reader

In many middle schools, students might go through a day without anyone ever asking them what they did over the weekend, how their siblings are doing, or what presents they received for their birthday. Taking time to pay attention to the social and emotional lives of our students is just as important as assessing their ability to read and learn and apply content. We need to teach the whole child if we expect the whole child to respond to us. So when we ask them to be good readers and writers and thinkers and invest in getting to know the rest of what makes them *them*, their investment in learning our content grows.

Notice Lydia's growing honesty and enthusiasm as she writes about her reading:

Lydia: I'm so glad we do a lot of reading during class because at home I'm usually busy, so I don't get to read a lot. But I'm ALMOST . . . done with "Perks of Being a Wallflower"! I feel like I'm taking forever to read it but that's ok. After "Perks of Being a Wallflower" I want to read "Because of Winn Dixie" because in fifth grade my teacher read it to us but I want to read it by myself. I'm really glad I'm liking reading this year because reading has always been a struggle for me. It has really helped me as a reader! I cant wait till I'm done with this book, I have so many books in mind that I really want to read! If you have any more book suggestions make sure you let me know so I can write them down.

Teacher: I'm so happy that you are enjoying reading again! It sounds like you are beginning to think beyond the book you are reading, too. Setting reading goals for yourself. Keep it up! Great to see you so enthusiastic and willing to read on your own. Besides talking about books Lydia, what do you spend most of your time doing outside of school? Do you have anything about which you are truly passionate? Do you have a favorite band or artist? Favorite song? What do you do with yourself when you have time off from school? What would a perfect day look like for you? Looking forward to reading your answer!! We will let you know (about other books you could try reading)! I just remembered a book called "It's Kind of a Funny Story" by Ned Vizzini. I feel like it's a similar style to Perks, but it might be a little more modern.

When eighth graders are asked how much independent reading they do outside of class, their answer is nearly always a subdued "not much" or "very little" or "none at all." Most say that they do not have much free time anymore, or that other things grab their attention at home, or that reading is not the thing that jumps to the front of their minds when they are relaxing. There are many and varied challenges associated with the middle school routine: forty-three-minute classes; increasing amounts of homework; sports; dance or music lessons every other night; competitions or hockey tournaments on the weekends; video games; cell phones; social media—the list goes on and on.

And the schedules only seem to get more and more complex as the grades progress.

Ten minutes of daily independent reading might not seem like much, but it is the start and spark that many middle-level readers need to turn them back on to reading, remind them what reading may have been like back in elementary school when days stretched on forever and life was less chaotic and complicated. Lydia appreciates the ten minutes she gets, and believe it or not, assuming she has been in school most days in September, Lydia will have already surpassed four hours of reading time by early October!

So the fact that Lydia is "getting to like reading this year" is not surprising especially considering that she feels "busy" outside of school. As September turns to October, readers enjoy the ten minutes of reading at the start of class more and more not only as a chance to read from a book of their choosing but also as a restful activity, one that gives their bodies a chance to get away from the business, busy-ness, and drama of the day, to reset, decompress, regroup. In order to get the most out of reading, the body must be in a state of quiet focus, tuning out the world and deliberately tuning in to the text.

Like mindfulness, reading is a practice that gets easier the more we engage. With each passing school day, readers are able to enter their texts more quickly and for longer stretches of time. Lydia is liking reading more because she is getting better (and quicker) at focusing her attention on the book in her hands. She is more adept at entering and exiting a text. This skill can only be sharpened through consistent, regular reading time and a willingness to stay engaged and become more resilient.

Many of us are well aware of the buzz around mindfulness in the classroom these days. And why not? Being reflective thinkers and learners is a skill that extends far beyond the classroom walls. The fact that we are asking our students to become more aware of what and how and why they are learning, to become more aware of how to regulate feelings and stress, is not only appropriate but also a necessary and integral part of a learner's (and reader's) overall development.

Learning to read well and reading independently encourages a more engaged and focused state; it encourages, for some, the examination of what it means to read, to think more deliberately about the internal processes associated with making meaning from text. Whether conscious or not, independent readers work to regulate and relax their internal state as they move toward automaticity.

Allowing students regular opportunities to read on their own throughout the school day means providing time for increasing awareness and self-regulation, time to settle the body, focus the mind, decompress, and adjust. Time to reflect and monitor and reassess. Independent reading can be a self-aware, contemplative practice in these ways, with the added benefit of learning new words, gaining new perspective, and building a larger, more diverse base of knowledge and experience.

All this is happening to Lydia this year.

Lydia: I finished "Perks of being a Wallflower"!!! I'm so happy it's like the first actual chapter book i have finished in like 6 months! I am now starting to read "Because of Winn-Dixie" I have read it before but I would like to read it again. I will most likely finish this one a bit faster because it has less words on each page. Outside of school I'm mostly with my friends. When I'm not with my friends I'm cleaning, organizing, or watching youtube. I love reading but I don't know how to fit it in my outside of school life. If I read at night I get super tired and end up stopping after a page, but if I read during the day I think about all the stuff I could be doing instead of reading. But I am going to try to start reading outside of school more.

Teacher: I am SO HAPPY that you are going to give reading a try outside of school, Lydia! I would keep trying to read before bed. Don't worry if you fall asleep after a page or two. This will happen at first until your body gets used to the idea of reading before bed. You will develop more and more reading stamina. Just keep at it! Don't give up, and I bet you will be reading 10 or 15 pages every night!

How is Because of Winn Dixie going? I got SO MUCH more out of that
book the second time through it. What are you loving about the book as
you read it for a second time? BTW, have you seen the movie?

So many good things that are happening in Lydia's reading life are evident in this entry. Most importantly, she is finishing books. Ten minutes of
reading a day has provided her with an opportunity to not only start but also
push through a book to its end. A book of her own choosing.

The confidence boost that readers receive from reaching the end of a book
cannot be measured. By finishing *Perks*, Lydia has proven to herself, her
teacher, and the world that she is capable of reading an entire book on her
own, that she is capable of understanding a text on her own, of utilizing a text
to think of her world in new and different ways.

She is excited about all of this (evident by her use of exclamation points!)
and is immediately thinking about her next book (*Because of Winn Dixie*) as
well as how she will read the next book ("most likely finish this one a bit
faster").

Lydia's growing awareness about what inhibits her ability to engage in
reading is also evident in this entry when she talks about her difficulty
finding time to read outside of class. She admits to falling asleep when she
tries to read at night. Her teacher lets her know that this is a common occur-
rence and that she should not be deterred, that reading is an introspective
activity, one that forces the body to slow down, and so, at first, sleep is a
good sign that a student is actually trying to slip into a reading state of mind.
Lydia is encouraged to keep working at it, keep trying to find time to read
outside of class, outside of school, starting with small chunks of time before
bed.

We can encourage all students to read outside of school by suggesting
(not assigning) independent reading for homework. Start by suggesting five
to ten minutes of reading for homework in September, and by the end of the
year, the reading time can progress to thirty to forty minutes per night. True,
not every student will do the reading every single night, but teachers can
continue to model the different places that reading can happen in the "real"
world: waiting rooms, car rides, sports study hall, bus trips, waiting to be
picked up by a parent, after dinner, in the cafeteria, after taking a test, weekend mornings and evenings, over breaks, on the beach, by the pool, in a tree
house, on the back patio, with a sibling or parent, with a teacher, in line at a
store.

The impact that regular independent reading time can have on our students is immense, and so it is stressed and promoted from day 1 to day 180.

Lydia is beginning to think about reading as a priority and is going to try
to start reading more outside of school. Music to a reading teacher's ears!

What happens when we ask students early on to describe their outside-of-school selves? Their likes and dislikes? Their passions? This is a reading teacher wanting as much information as possible on each individual student so as to better meet their literacy needs, to provide a more appropriate learning environment, to provide a more appropriate middle-level learning experience. To educate the whole child.

By understanding a reader's likes and dislikes, teachers can become more effective recommenders of books. Think about it: Sally dances six days a week; John takes apart computers for fun; Stella has twelve pets at home and takes care of them all on weekends; Carlos races go-karts all over the east coast (that's why he misses most Friday classes); Zoey plays volleyball, lacrosse, and softball and practices for travel basketball at night; Dominick takes care of his three siblings after school until his mom gets home (he is so tired by the time he gets in his bed that he can't even think about reading); Mario loves video games and plays four or five hours a night; Susan bakes for fun; Jarod is obsessed with his iPhone; and Brent loves the outdoors (hiking, mountain climbing, and camping). See table 19.1 for examples of book suggestions based on students' interests.

Having students write about their interests outside of school gives their teacher an advantage when they put on the hat of "Book Recommender." Being mindful of a student's likes and dislikes (and being able to look back at them often) allows a teacher to zero in much faster on books that match particular students. When Brent is on the hunt for a new book (or getting close to finishing a book), understanding that he loves the outdoors is crucial in keeping up his reading momentum, especially early in the year.

A quick Google search related to Young Adult survival books, Young Adult adventure books, Young Adult outdoors books, books like *Hatchet* by Gary Paulsen, or books like *My Side of the Mountain* by Jean Craighead George will likely provide a list of titles that would be right up Brent's alley. Being a great book recommender means knowing your readers and being mindful of their interests and needs.

Lydia: So, "Because of Winn-Dixie" is going GREAT! I'm actually almost done with it. I have about 20 more pages. I'm going to start reading at night instead of watching youtube. The next book I'm going to read is "Its Kind of a Funny Story" it seems like a really good book. Also I have not seen the movie to "Because of Winn-Dixie." I'm really excited that reading is working out for me this year. I'm a really slow reader but hopefully i can improve that this year. Do you know if they have "Its Kind of a Funny Story" at the library? If they do I'll probably go get it monday or tuesday because I'm sure I will finish this book by the end of the weekend.

Table 19.1. Books That Mr. Rose Suggests for Specific Students Based on What He Knows about Their Literacy Skills, Needs, Interests, Attitudes, and Prior Knowledge

Student	Books
Sally (dance)	*A Time to Dance* by Padma Venkatraman *I Wanna Be Where You Are* by Kristina Forest *Everywhere You Want to Be* by Christina June
John (computers)	*Willful Machines* by Tim Floreen *Where Future's End* by Parker Peevyhouse *My Brilliant Idea* by Stuart David
Stella (pets)	*Where the Red Fern Grows* by Wilson Rawles *Because of Winn Dixie* by Kate DiCamillo *Sounder* by William Armstrong *Beasts: What Animals Can Teach Us about the Origins of Good and Evil* by Jeffrey Moussaieff Masson
Carlos (go-carts)	*Saturday Night Dirt* by Will Weaver *Wolf by Wolf* by Ryan Graudin *Crash into You* by Katie McGarry
Zoey (sports)	*The Crossover* by Kwame Alexander *Gym Candy* by Carl Deuker *Whale Talk* by Chris Crutcher
Dominic (family)	*The Poet X* by Elizabeth Acevedo *I Am Not Your Perfect Mexican Daughter* by Erika L. Sánchez *Tyler Johnson Was Here* by Jay Coles *I Am Alfonso Jones* by Tony Medina, illustrated by Stacey Robinson and John Jennings
Mario (video games)	*Ready Player One* by Ernest Cline *Epic* by Conor Kostick *The Eye of Mind* by James Dashner
Susan (baking)	*A La Carte* by Tanita S. Davis *Bittersweet* by Sarah Ockler *From Where I Watch You* by Shannon Grogan
Jarod (iPhones)	*Dear Evan Hansen* by Val Emmich, with Steven Levenson, and Justin Paul *The Tech-Wise Family: Everyday Steps for Putting Technology in Its Proper Place* by Andy Crouch *12 Ways Your Phone Is Changing You* by Tony Reinke
Brent (outdoors)	*Hatchet* by Gary Paulsen *Holes* (Holes Series) by Louis Sachar *My Side of the Mountain* by Jean Craighead George

Teacher: No way!!! I am such a proud teacher right now (in response to "I'm going to start reading at night"). So glad you like it [*Winn Dixie*]!!! One of my favorites, too. I think they might (have the book in the library).

Not sure. You could definitely borrow it from the high school library. Did you finish *Winn Dixie*? Do you want to read another dog book? I have soooooooo many titles of dog books to share with you (ones where the dog dies at the end and ones where the dog lives!). Let me know how your reading is going and if you need help finding a new book. . . . Talk to you soon.

Did you finish *Winn Dixie* yet, Lydia? I think you did, because I saw that you started a different book. . . . (no response)

Lydia has been absent now for an extended period of time, and her teacher is unsure why this is.

Teacher: We have missed you in class the last couple of days, Lydia. Hope everything is going OK for you. I hope you are still giving yourself chances to read. If you get a chance, tell me about the book you are reading now. Where did you get it? Why is it a good book for you? What are you getting out of reading the book?

Lydia: The reasons I have been out are due to mostly doctors appointments and dentist appointments. . . . I also had an incident at school with another girl. . . . I did finish Winn Dixie. It was a GREAT book and easy read! Thank you guys for being so patient with me because of me being out. I am now reading "It's Kind of a Funny Story" I couldn't find it in the library and the librarian couldn't borrow it from the high school, but _____ heard me talking about it and let me borrow it! I'm not that far in it I just finished the first chapter.

Teacher: So happy you liked this book!! The author, Kate DiCamillo, has other books. When you are done with *Funny Story*, maybe you can read another by the *Winn Dixie* author. . . . I'm glad to see you back in school.

Self-awareness is a two-way street with the online Reading Conversation Journal. Students become more aware of their reading process, habits, preferences, and experiences, while the teacher becomes more mindful of his students, their abilities and interests, and his approach to teaching them. In the exchanges above, the teacher notices that Lydia has missed class for an extended period of time and recognizes that to be the best reader she can be, Lydia must be in the proper frame of mind. Her teacher acknowledges her missing class, giving her a chance to "clear the air" of any unnecessary baggage before turning the conversation back to books. Notice that her teacher provides a positive support system rather than reprimanding or penalizing as a response to her chronic absences.

Chapter Twenty

Weekly Check and Connect

How many times do students miss class, only to come back two or three days later with no explanation or no time to explain? The Reading Conversation Journal provides a weekly "check and connect" time for teacher and student, a time to catch up and feed the deep-rooted connections that will grow steadily month by month through the school year, fostering the kind of reading (and learning) that does not stop come June, but continues throughout the teenage years and then the college/work years and finally into adulthood.

We see with Lydia's example that the bonds forged in these conversations with her teacher could be long lasting and long term. Her teacher is most mindful of this overriding goal: to build independent, lifelong readers. It is the overriding goal of the school year.

Lydia: I am on the 6th chapter of "It's Kind of a Funny Story" It's been really great! It definitely reminds me of "Perks of Being a Wallflower" just in a different format. I have been doing good with my reading at home and it has been helping me go to sleep easier and faster. I am excited to actually read this year and enjoy it! Also i really like the outsiders book. You definitely see it another way when someone is reading it to you instead of you reading it yourself. I am really sad that miss West is leaving soon. . . . The student teacher in french left yesterday to go back to France but at least shes coming back at the end of january. Well if you have any more book suggestions at any time please let me know because i'd love to put more books down on my list!

Teacher: I agree. Why do you think the book is different when it is read out loud by someone? Let me know when you are ready! I have A TON! Lol

Lydia continues to show increased confidence with regard to genre selection as well as increased motivation to read outside of class. There is also the added benefit of independent reading when Lydia comments that reading has been "helping [her] go to sleep easier and faster." That she notices this and knows this about herself will help in her future reading situations.

Reading and RCJs can be perceived as a form of relaxation. What a fantastic outlet to offer busy students consumed with increased class loads and homework, extracurricular activities and nightly practices, electronic watches and girlfriends and boyfriends and nosy parents and screen time and televisions and texting, video games, social media, and smartphones.

Regular. Independent. Reading. Time. In class. The eye at the center of the storm. One of the greatest gifts teachers can give.

Chapter Twenty-One

The Reading Conversation Journal

A Critical Look

Some readers might be wondering about Lydia's responses at this point. Are these responses truly the equivalent of the kind of high-quality literary analysis essays and papers required by most middle and high school language arts curricula? Are these responses *really* helping to prepare Lydia for high school and collegiate essays along with state tests, SATs, and college entrance exams?

It's great that Lydia is getting more comfortable with picking out her own books, and it's nice that she is going to miss the student teacher, and it is clear that she is enjoying reading more, but is that enough? Where's the deep literary analysis? Where's the comparing and contrasting of different books and genres? Where's the vocabulary instruction, the end-of-the-chapter questions, the five-paragraph essay, the *grammar lessons*!?

Good questions.

This Reading *Conversation* Journal (not reading-*response* journal) is intended to satisfy a very specific need in classrooms at all levels. Students often enter the classroom disillusioned in terms of independent reading, firm in their belief that reading (especially reading outside of the classroom) serves no real purpose. The act of reading for pleasure or enjoyment or some other reason is no longer fun and is either nonexistent in students' lives or, at best, very low on the priority meter of the middle-level student.

This phenomenon is perplexing and troubling. How can eighth-grade students already have lost the desire to read? How can so many say that they don't read books or barely ever read unless it is assigned? It is clear to any middle-level teacher that the majority of their students can read, so why won't they?

Most teachers of literacy realize that they can get these students to love reading again if they could only sit down with them, talk to them, encourage them, motivate them. But there are so many of them (over one hundred students most years)! That's over one hundred readers that we must talk to and encourage and cajole and coax, one hundred readers with which we need to connect and get real, one hundred readers we have to convince that reading is indeed worthwhile and beneficial not only in the moment but also in the future and, well, *forever*. And all of this convincing needs to be done quickly and regularly.

Hence, the birth of the online Reading Conversation Journal—a way teachers can start talking (in real, unobstructed, relatively uninfluenced language) to their students about real, authentic self-selected reading in an unfiltered, uninhibited, low-stress environment.

And the RCJ is flexible, *so flexible*! Teachers can decide (finally) when and if to ask readers to do things like:

- read a classic;
- read two (or three) books at once;
- reread a childhood favorite;
- select a book from the library;
- keep track of the books read in one month;
- read an entire series;
- read a book then watch the movie;
- watch the movie then read the book;
- read a book under one hundred pages;
- read a book over one thousand pages;
- read a book recommended by a friend;
- read a book with a parent or sibling;
- read a book with a favorite teacher;
- sign up for a library card;
- ask for a book for a present;
- summarize the book in fifteen or fewer sentences, ten or less, five or less;
- summarize the book in one sentence, and much more!

And we can attempt to reach *every* reader. Not just the ones who read well and want to read. Not just the ones who hesitate to read or hate reading. *All* readers.

Every reader is different. Each reader wants (and needs) a different conversation depending on their reading history, their reading goals, and their motivation and willingness to want to read. The RCJ gives teachers a fighting chance to meet (or at least address) the needs of all one hundred of their readers, once a week, every week. The RCJ can be the ultimate engagement activity: one hundred chances to teach reading each week, one hundred different needs, one hundred chances to reconnect, to motivate, to confide in, to move.

One week a teacher might ask one student to write an entry comparing Holden Caulfield's relationship with Phoebe in *The Catcher in the Rye* to Ponyboy Curtis's relationship with Johnny Cade in *The Outsiders*, and for another student (in the same class) the teacher might explain what the red squiggly lines mean under typed words in Google Docs. The teacher is giving each reader exactly what that reader needs.

Every student is reading what they want to read when they want to read it (for the most part). Every student is setting their own reading goals, moving at a comfortable pace, constantly being monitored and encouraged to read more often both in and outside of school.

In short, Lydia is getting exactly what she needs at this time in her reading development. She has basically moved from an unmotivated non-reader, to a reader excited about the literary possibilities before her. Books are opening up a whole new world for Lydia.

Lydia is on her way, we hope, to lifelong reading.

Chapter Twenty-Two

Conversations as Ongoing Assessment

Continuous Monitoring and Adjusting

Don't forget, too, that the journal is a once-a-week activity. The reading is mostly happening outside of the classroom (except for the ten minutes of reading at the start of every class). So there is much more going on in the classroom each day than just independent reading and conversation journals. The rest of the class time is full of the kind of reading and writing activities and lessons that we might expect a middle school classroom to house. The online journal is just one piece of an entire language arts curriculum puzzle. A *big* piece, yes. A *very* big piece. But just one piece.

Much more teaching and learning happens outside of the journal. From explicit writing instruction in genres like narrative, poetry, literary essay, and research articles to deep literary analysis and shared reading experiences, the possibilities for reading and writing instruction are endless beyond of the RCJ, and it's good to know that the conversation journal only takes about a class period per week.

Up to this point, the journal has been required each week, but the responses have come about with relatively *no strings attached*. This is by design.

After years of data collection from student surveys, we have found that one of the main reasons students are turned off to reading by eighth grade is because reading now seems to come with associated teacher-created requirements—worksheets, book reports, text-based questions, short-answer essay questions, end-of-chapter reviews, chapter quizzes, mid-point check sheets, vocabulary checks, reader-response journals, summary sheets, character charts. "Reading is always followed by *something*," students say. "All that *stuff* ruins reading."

That is not to say that reading should never be followed by checks for understanding. In no way is this book trying to downplay the importance of the list of creative and meaningful ways teachers assess students' understanding and help them think more deeply and more analytically about the texts that they read.

Rather, we are suggesting that there need not be strings attached to *all* reading done inside and outside of school. Students should be permitted, at some point, to read relatively free of constraints and from material of their own choosing.

So we must be careful with how much we require our readers to do. The overriding goal is always to create and mold lifelong readers, and so this online journal must feel and look more like a free and open conversation, an exchange of ideas with the student as the guide. Teachers can help students get excited about reading again, excited about books and what they have to offer. We can influence students like Lydia, students who want to read.

However, teachers can acquire feedback every now and then from our readers, and so we can take time to ask readers about certain aspects of the online journal and about our class:

- How do students like having ten minutes of reading time every day?
- How do they feel they are showing reading growth?
- What are their reading goals for the remainder of the year?

These are the same questions Nancie Atwell (2014) invites teachers to ask themselves as they plan and assess their literacy programs.

The answers to these inquiries can provide valuable information on how to move forward with the journal while also continuing to give students a chance to take the reins with regard to their own learning and growth. As students become more mindful of their reading process and skill development, they also become more engaged and confident in the whole reading experience. Confidence breeds motivation. Here are Lydia's replies:

Lydia: Reading for 10 minutes everyday has really improved my reading skills. I feel like i can kind of pay more attention to the text instead of what's going through my mind. Also responding in this journal has maybe kind of helped. I am not sure but it helps me because i can ask for book suggestions or let you know how i am doing on my books. My reading habits have changed. I used to never read. I always hated it because i would read a page then forget everything i read, so i would get really frustrated. But now i read a lot more and actually enjoy reading. I want to improve me (my) reading speed but that might just take time. I also want to improve the way i write, like the words i use. I kind of use "baby" words so i hope i can improve on that.

Teacher: Great, Lydia! So happy (and proud!)!

Yes—keep reading at your own pace (so that you remember what you have read). You will read faster eventually—it just takes time.

Through her answers to her teacher's inquiries, we can start to sense a real transformation in Lydia as a reader. She refers to her reading focus and attentiveness when she says that she can "pay more attention to the text instead of what's going through my mind." She recognizes that the online RCJ gives her a way to "ask for book suggestions" and "let [the teacher] know how I am doing on books."

Lydia assesses herself as a reader and notices that her habits have changed in just five short months of school, that she feels like she *enjoys* reading more and that she is *choosing* to read more now than she did before. She finishes her self-assessment by setting some goals for herself—to read "faster."

This focus on and attention to her literacy growth and development, her reading behaviors and habits, is what's going to propel Lydia through the remainder of her year of independent reading. She has been awakened to her reading body and mind and is more in control of what and how she reads, where and when she reads best, and maybe most importantly, what she needs to do to push through, to move forward in this process. Perhaps the enjoyment she experiences as she immerses herself in stories will make the reading process effortless.

Lydia has adopted a sense of reading urgency and a sense that reading is so much more than just a required school task. She is starting to recognize reading for what it truly is: the vehicle by which she can travel anywhere—in her mind and in her life. *Books for Living* by Will Schwalbe (2017) contains excellent essays that support this notion of slowing down and finding inspiration and connections between reading and life.

Lydia: So, i'm a little over the half point of "its Kind of a Funny Story." i'm pretty proud to have got this far in my book. It has kind of took me a while but thats okay. I usually don't read "big" books because i will usually quit in the middle, but i'm going to push through this book because i really like it. Next i think i am going to read "The House of the Scorpion." Lately i have not been reading at home but now that i got my backpack back from _____ i am going to start taking my book home. I think i'm going to read at my desk instead of my bed because if i am in my bed i tend to want to lay down. Tonight i am going to push to read for 20–30 minutes. So i will let you know how that goes on Monday!

In the end, it is hard not to want to stand up and cheer for Lydia. She has obviously come so far as a reader this year, and she still has another half of a year to go. She sets the intention of changing where she reads so that she doesn't fall asleep while reading. She's able to make this choice and express it and learn about herself because of her participation in the Reading Conversation Journal each week.

In this final written entry, Lydia is showing confidence ("I'm proud to have got this far in my book") and resilience ("I'm going to push through") as well as mindfulness about where she will read in the future to make her reading time more efficient ("I think I am going to read at my desk instead of my bed"). She is also setting her own reading goals ("read for 20–30 minutes") and looking ahead with energy and exuberance, knowing that she has someone who will share in this meaningful experience with her ("will let you know how that goes on Monday").

This is a student who will hopefully read for life; this is a student who will hopefully learn for life. She has shown in her conversations that she has developed both engagement and self-awareness as a reader to help her do this.

FINAL THOUGHTS

This part of our book introduced us to Lydia, a student very different from Kaylee—whom we met in part II—in that Lydia is somewhat harder to get to know and assess as a reader and writer. Without the online conversation with Lydia, her teacher would have a tough time relating to her in any tangible way, given the great number of students he teaches on a daily basis. Through Lydia's words, he finds a nonreader who has become more self-aware through the process of becoming an engaged reader and writer. The back-and-forth exchange between teacher and student reinforces a trusting, easy relationship that fosters continuous dialogue, increased engagement, and the newly found self-awareness as a literacy learner.

Appendix

*A Dozen Questions Teachers Ask about Using the RCJ as
an Integral Part of Their Comprehensive Reading and
Writing Program*

Talk deepens thinking and learning.—Gallagher and Kittle (2018)

OVERVIEW

The four parts of this book have shown how online Reading Conversation
Journals have taken hold in one classroom for hundreds of eighth graders.
Part I introduced the concept, practical aspects, and value of online RCJs as
well as our beliefs about literacy learning.

Part II took a deep dive into one ongoing conversation between Kaylee
and her teacher, a conversation that helps illustrate how motivation, confidence, and trust between student and teacher can be developed over a sustained period of time through writing about reading. Engaging in conversation with this young reader and studying her entries help us recognize the
importance of confidence and motivation for building independent readers—
readers willing and eager to pick up texts during their own free time and of
their own free will for their own unique purposes.

Part III offered a new way of defining "text" and showed how teachers
can find diverse texts easily and quickly as they differentiate for a range of
learners. In part IV we demonstrated how RCJs help students become more
cognitively aware of their own literacy interests, habits, growth, and goals.

Throughout the book we provide examples of students' journal responses,
as well as the teacher's written responses to student responses, including

some analysis of or "meta-talk" about these exchanges. Our meta-talk often reveals the teacher's specific and intentional teaching and the subsequent learning that was taking place for both teacher and student within the selected teacher-student conversation.

Now we're ready to answer some pointed questions about the online Reading Conversation Journal, questions asked by reading and writing teachers at all levels—locally, statewide, and nationally—as we deliver professional development that promotes holistic, student-centered literacy practices. This section addresses several questions that teachers wonder about—both the smaller details of how to implement RCJs in their own classrooms and the larger, more theoretical issues regarding why we believe in and utilize the RCJ.

QUESTION 1: SHOULD THE READING CONVERSATION JOURNALS BE GRADED? IF SO, HOW? WHAT DOES YOUR RECORD-KEEPING LOOK LIKE?

The tension between formal grading of student writing and getting students to write with passion, authentic expression, and risk (not to mention joy) is real and palpable. Students do not write with the same unbridled emotion when they know that there will be a grade attached. The fact that students ask, "Will this be graded?" before they start writing is a good indication that they have two different ways of approaching school writing—the graded way and the ungraded way.

The online RCJ was originally a classroom inquiry project implemented as a way of collecting more evidence that reading instruction was effective, a method that provided regular indicators that students were growing in their literacy skills and dispositions. It was intentionally created as a weekly journal activity, an informal, ungraded assessment, a place for readers and writers to express their original ideas about reading and writing and about life.

Instinctively, teachers sometimes realize that requiring *less* actually yields *more*. That is, by not restricting readers to read a certain number of books or pages or paragraphs per day, per week, and per year, and by not requiring students to write x number of sentences or paragraphs each time they sit down to write, or to write their entries in a certain way following a strict rubric or formula, students will likely produce more authentic reader responses. We also know that students will probably read more if they choose what to read, as opposed to always reading what the teacher selects. All of the above assumptions proved correct!

Pressures associated with grading and assessment in the world of public education abound. With the advent of online, real-time grading programs and systems, a teacher's assignments, curriculum structure, and grading philosophies are suddenly on display, out into the open, in plain sight, for students, parents, other teachers, and administrators to see and critique. Gone are the days of the handheld, green-covered grade book, full of first and last names, check marks, private letter grades, and teacher comments.

Data-driven instruction and standards-based assessments, coupled with the push to standardize curriculum and increase math and ELA test scores, have shined a spotlight directly on reading and writing instruction and the ability of teachers to show measurable student literacy growth and development. Across the state of New York, for example, "underperforming" reading and writing districts are being asked to provide detailed answers as to why their state assessment scores are low, and why their school's growth is not matching up with similar schools and districts at the state and national level.

In response, districts have a renewed level of interest and intensity directed toward the quality of reading and writing instruction that is happening in their classrooms. Teachers in all subject areas are incorporating daily literacy objectives into their lessons, in addition to knowing which students are performing below the reading assessment benchmark and providing appropriate interventions.

And, of course, all good instruction in reading and writing comes with an assessment plan, right?

What can we do in our classrooms to ensure that every student not only shows growth in the skillsets associated with reading and writing, but also shows growth on state reading and writing exams and assessments, which ultimately become the indicator of a school district's progress? And then, how do we assess this reading and writing growth in a way that does not undermine the teaching and learning and risk-taking and confidence-building that are happening in the classroom?

Visits from state officials, development of ELA curriculum committees, attempts to standardize literacy instruction, trips to nearby high-performing schools, districtwide book studies, faculty meetings focused on best practices in reading instruction, incorporation of literacy coaches, extra reading instructors, gap analysis focused on the skills associated with the most missed questions on the state ELA and STAR exams, and the continuous and laborious collection and analysis of mountains of data—all have been school districts' attempt to answer the above questions. Is it working?

Most teachers (and administrators too) have felt numerous pressures when it comes to grading readers and writers. When grades went "online," the pressure only increased, leaving many feeling like they needed to "prove" their curriculum, their teaching, and their homework philosophies. How many grades should a teacher have for a ten-week marking period? One a week? Three a week? Ten a week? More? Does everything a student produces need a grade?

What if our graded assignments do not match the other ELA teachers' assignments in the department or building? What if parents question the grading procedures? What if administrators demand they grade more often? What if teachers judge each other based on the grades they are putting into the online system and compare themselves to other reading and writing teachers? Decisions about grading have far-reaching implications.

And what about the students? How do they feel about being graded on their reading and writing work? Students often act and write differently when they know that they are being graded or judged. We do not want students' writing to go from meaningful and raw, honest and engaging back to formulaic and robotic. How can any teacher truly satisfy everyone involved in the grading process? How can we ensure that our students continue to write meaningfully about texts while also acknowledging that students are not the only ones interested in the reading and writing grades they are receiving?

The answer is simple: compromise.

The grading policy and practices for the Reading Conversation Journal asks students to write regularly, to make up entries that are missed, and to write in increasingly elaborate and complex ways about the texts they choose to read throughout the school year. Very simple.

Ideally, the journal should be a true "no strings attached" literacy assignment, one in which students write freely and naturally about the texts with which they engage. Student surveys at the start of every eighth-grade year indicate that students are the most familiar (and the most comfortable) writing from a prompt attached to an article, poem, or narrative excerpt. Students come to school at the beginning of the year fairly adept at writing claim statement essays and short-answer responses based on a one- to three-page article. Students are well versed in using evidence in these short essays, and even citing the evidence using line and page numbers.

Teachers appreciate students' skill at writing in this "on demand" manner. Tightly structured reading-response writing can be a part of all ELA and other curricula, but as mentioned before, we need greater balance. We need to offer students more writing with fewer steadfast rules, writing a little less reliant on tightly structured paragraphs and citations and writing with the idea at the top of the page that will bring surprises and possibilities that no one can predict.

The RCJ is a nice contrast to the strict methodology of the typical response essay. Even the name, "Reading Conversation Journal," promotes writing as a less restrictive composition that encourages the elaboration and growth of readers' original ideas as they manipulate, struggle with, and extrapolate the meaning of not only the texts that they read but also the process by which they make meaning when they read. Of course there are also several other types of writing expected during the school year that *do* require students to follow more rigorous criteria. Thus, the need for balance.

So, to answer the question more directly, students can be "graded" on their conversation journal entries if and when the teacher feels a need to have this activity documented and in order to track growth across time, but the grading can be simple and matter-of-fact. In the first five weeks, students can be encouraged to write about what they are reading, gaining credit for every entry written, *no matter the length or style of the response.*

Every student writes their weekly entry, in class, and they are expected to make up any missed entry. The points they receive could be equivalent to about 10–20 percent of their overall grade for the quarter. The teacher can put a grade every two weeks or so (for a total of two to four RCJ grades per quarter). This system allows for the journal to count without dedicating too much weight to it for the overall marking period grade.

QUESTION 2: WHAT INSTRUCTION DOES THE TEACHER OFFER BEFORE STUDENTS WRITE IN THEIR JOURNALS ON FRIDAYS?

First, we want to share with you that our next book will take a close look at how this teacher teaches reading and writing skills and strategies throughout the week, some lessons that support the RCJ, and some lessons that support the many other reading/writing projects going on in his classroom at the same time. The scope of this book is too narrow to include this material. But here is some of what the teacher does before students journal online.

Before students read and write on Fridays, their teacher provides explicitly modeled mini-lessons. Some mini-lessons are designed to help students manage the technological aspects of and tips for maintaining the conversation journal, while other mini-lessons support, model, and reinforce students' reading and writing skills and elevate their ability to write reader responses. Examples of mini-lessons include:

1. dating and numbering your entry;
2. writing the newest entry at the top of the document;
3. answering questions/prompts posed by the teacher;
4. writing about reading challenges and successes;
5. how to follow a link in your journal;
6. how to write about the process of finding great books;
7. writing about reading focus and stamina;
8. writing about the difficulties associated with reading outside of school;
9. identifying favorite genres and authors;
10. writing about characters' actions and pivotal plot moments;
11. writing about dialogue; and
12. writing about characteristics of great writing.

The teacher knows which skills he needs to teach each week based on the individual entries he is reading and responding to all week; he knows their reading and writing needs because he's in touch with each of them regularly. Students also receive a handout of optional writing stems that can help scaffold their response writing, in case they have a hard time getting started:

- I am starting to notice . . .
- I am wondering about . . .
- One thing that is confusing me is . . .
- Something that stands out in this text is . . .
- One thing I am noticing about myself as a reader is . . .
- This (or this part of the) book is interesting because . . .

You might use exemplary student journal entries as models right before students begin composing their journal entry on Friday, pointing out the great characteristics of the model entry. You could say things like, "Look at the way Cindy has separated her ideas into paragraphs," or, "Notice how Jamal is asking questions about the book that he is reading," or, "Does everyone see how Malic first summarizes what is happening in his book and then answers the questions the teacher asked?"

Good literacy teachers will also write (and talk) about the texts they are reading. Modeling and talking through your own thoughts and ideas related to your own reading and your own response writing will have the greatest impact on students moving their responses to a new level. Writing your own reading responses every now and then also reminds us how complex and challenging the task is, how much thought and effort go into a meaningful reading-response entry.

Above all, students must read more than they ever have *during any* year of schooling thus far. Allowing for structured reading time in class every day (ten minutes minimum) and suggesting choice book reading "homework" every night (and on weekends) will encourage voluminous reading. Another idea would be to start the year with ten minutes of reading a night and increase the reading homework by one minute per week (so that students are ideally reading forty minutes a day during the final week of school).

QUESTION 3: ARE STUDENTS ASSIGNED INDEPENDENT READING FOR HOMEWORK?

The word *homework* is used here, but really, you could call it "after-school work." Naming many of our own competing demands for attention, you can talk to students about how difficult it can be for us to actually find reading time outside of school. Encourage students to list their distractions and time-eaters so they might begin to gain more awareness and control over making reading more of a priority outside of school.

You might ask yourself at this point what you believe about homework. What are your homework practices, and why do you require them? Is homework a necessary part of school? Why or why not? What purposes does homework serve? Do we have concrete evidence that homework leads to increased student achievement? Is assigning homework equitable for all students?

Teachers can assign, encourage, and talk about reading outside the classroom on a daily basis. Even with our unrelenting encouragement, will every single student read every single night? Of course not. Not at first, anyway. But we know that if we can get even 50 or 60 percent of our students reading regularly (three or four times a week), we will be doing them a *huge* service as they move forward in their schooling, educational, and work careers.

In addition to reinforcing the importance of developing a regular reading routine, you might consider identifying your own independent reading habits. How do you fit reading into your busy schedule outside of school? Do you carry a book everywhere you go, reading in lines, reading in parking lots, reading in waiting rooms, reading before orchestra and dance concerts, listening to audiobooks in the car? How often do you read and for what purposes?

This teacher uses a "Reading Challenge," a year-long scavenger hunt that pushes readers to complete fifty or so tasks related to independent reading outside of school. You might give students small rewards if you "spy" on them reading out in public. Kind of like finding Waldo—you want to catch students in the act of reading outside of school, in the community, in the public eye. Rewards can range from special limited edition bookmarks to small gift cards to the local bookstore. Here are ten examples of reading challenges:

- Read a book in one sitting.
- Check a book out of the local library (and read it).
- Read a graphic novel.
- Ask for a book for a birthday or holiday present.
- Read a book with a friend.
- Read a book to a sibling or a pet.
- Read a classic.
- Read a book, and then watch the movie.
- Read a picture book.
- Read a series.

And now for the bad news: In their meta-analysis of thousands of research studies, Fisher, Frey, and Hattie (2016) found that, at the middle school level, there is a relatively small correlation between homework and student achievement (effect size = .30). Overall, despite what we may believe, homework has little impact on student learning. Assigning grades to students should be a purposeful decision made by each teacher for each assignment. The benefits of assigning a grade must outweigh the drawbacks for a particular piece of student work and for particular students given their unique academic, social, and emotional needs, strengths, and challenges.

It is not advisable to just assign grades to everything students submit. This practice is not only taxing on our valuable time but also not reflective of best practice. Choosing deliberately what goes into our grade book, those quarterly marks that are intended to reflect what each student knows and can do in your classroom, is a complex process that cannot be taken lightly. Grades follow a student through a whole academic career, and our role is to fully support each and every learner to the best of our ability, offering numerous ways they can demonstrate our learning targets. Choose wisely.

Teachers are answering to so many individuals (administrators, parents, counselors, doctors, therapists, after-school program directors, coaches, special education teachers, teaching assistants, academic intervention service instructors, superintendents, and even state education department officials) who want to know the number (or letter) that defines a single student as a reader. This task is nearly impossible and not at all student-centered given the complex nature of reading and the many factors involved in teaching reading to each individual child.

How can one number grade at the end of ten weeks be an accurate representation of a student's entire reading and writing progress?

In any given marking period, here is a list of just a few considerations a teacher thinks about as he grades each student and that student's ability as a reader/writer: How does this student create ideas and sustain written thought, space their writing out to control the pace of the reader, master common punctuation, select appropriate reading material, identify plot structure and character motivation, elaborate a complex thought or idea, string together cohesive sentences and paragraphs, identify characteristics of great writing, utilize mentor texts to help inform their own writing?

How does this student utilize deliberate revision to raise the level of their writing, summarize large chunks of text, respond adequately to on-demand reading prompts? How do they generate original writing ideas, sustain a narrative, use and understand figurative language and how it helps writing, motivate themselves to read and write, sustain focus and build reading and writing stamina, know when to put a book back on the shelf, know where to find more challenging texts, find the deeper meaning in a text? A tall order!

It is important to note here again that we do not favor one way of writing over another. Both ways of writing are equally important, but the formulaic, safe, teacher-controlled, rubric-centered, graded way of writing should not always take precedence over other less restricted, ungraded forms of classroom writing. ELA classrooms, we believe, should strive to reach a balance of the two forms arrived through careful, purposeful decision-making, planning, and reflection.

QUESTION 4: HOW LONG DOES IT TAKE TO READ AND RESPOND EACH WEEK?

The short answer is about an hour for every twenty journals, or roughly five minutes per journal entry. Wait, don't stop reading! Don't give up on the RCJ yet! There is a longer, more informative answer here.

At first, it sounds like a lot of time. Teachers will probably ask: Where could I *ever* find the time to do that? Teachers can think about the time spent on the journal not as *new* time *added* to the already overflowing schedule, but time *replacing* all the other attempts to try to motivate, mold, and move readers.

This list of often-tried (and failed) attempts to get readers talking about their books includes (but is not limited to) book reports, book reviews, book conferences, book circles, student-designed book trailers, book slideshows, student-led book discussions, book conferences, designing and asking students to respond to and then grading text-dependent questions and/or depth-of-knowledge questions and/or essay and/or compare/contrast essay questions, book webquests, author studies, read aloud and respond, draw a scene from the book, design a Facebook page for a character, journal writing prompts, diary entries, write a new chapter, and so on.

This also includes partner reading, student reading logs and charts and diagrams, and sticky note questions and sticky note journals and text-tagging . . . and then, of course, comes the *grading* of any one of the above response methods (or combination of any of the above).

The point is that teachers are *already* spending exorbitant amounts of time prepping, arranging the classroom, preparing groups and lists of students, finding appropriate reading materials, composing appropriate questions, and trying to get readers responding to the choice (and class) books that they read. Countless before- and after-school hours—with limited success. Small return on investment.

The reading levels in our classes are also growing so far apart! It is becoming increasingly difficult to get every student responding to texts in a way that is challenging for each student, but also not mind-numbingly boring and repetitive. In any given eighth-grade classroom, we can find a combination of college-level readers, students reading on grade level, students reading below grade level, and even a few truly beginning reading and writers just learning to decode multisyllabic words and compose complete simple sentences.

How can teachers design a reading-response activity, lesson, or unit that ensures each of these twenty-plus students is not only engaged, motivated, and feeling confident enough to complete the activity, but also challenged and able to learn and grow at their own pace, all the while attending to every student's social-emotional learning needs?

The Reading Conversation Journal is flexible enough to encompass this ever-changing, ultra-demanding, elastic twenty-first-century literacy student in need of meaningful personal connection, as well as specific, fine-tuned reading and writing instruction. The Reading Conversation Journal combines the most successful aspects of all of the above reading-response methods while also allowing teachers the chance to tailor their teaching in an attempt to meet the needs of *all* students in the classroom.

Once a week, through the RCJ, there comes another chance to reach every reader, every writer—another chance to connect, to teach, to redirect and motivate, to reflect, to play, to joke. Chances to recommend, to question, to stimulate, to mold and move . . . or on the best day, a chance to do all of those things.

In short, reading and responding to these weekly entries is time well spent.

QUESTION 5: HOW CAN TEACHERS DEVELOP A MORE DIVERSE CLASSROOM LIBRARY?

A teacher's classroom library is an essential component in all classrooms, but probably even more so in the English teacher's room. As teachers, we can talk about books forever, but unless we have the titles to back up our talk, our readers are bound to lose motivation and momentum with regard to independent reading.

With the help of our school librarian, we can fill our classrooms with current, diverse texts and genres that appeal to all types of readers: readers who connect with the LGBTQ community, readers of color, readers of a different culture, readers struggling with depression or divorce, readers who play sports, readers with disorders or difficult home lives, readers who move a lot, readers being raised by grandparents or siblings.

Our classroom libraries can appeal to readers with a physical disability, readers with a mental disability, readers who need pictures to help visualize, readers who would like to catch up on some classics, readers who feel lost, abandoned, alone, or unnoticed, readers who want to know more about history, readers who want to learn more about famous people, places, and events, and readers who don't like reading or are reluctant to pick up a book.

Teachers and librarians can collaborate regularly to provide a range of books for the classroom, keeping in mind that our students, most of whom live in white rural areas, will benefit from more exposure to texts by authors of color and authors from different cultures. The world is waiting for them!

Besides requesting books through your local librarian, there are other ways to build a diverse classroom library. Teachers can stop at book sales or garage sales, take student donations of books (parents are often looking to donate books), or utilize curriculum funds to buy books (if you are lucky enough to have funds available). Community literacy organizations run through local libraries, book stores, colleges, and YMCAs will often provide gently used books to schools free of charge or for a nominal fee.

The best thing a teacher can do to build a diverse, multi-genre classroom library is let everyone they know in on the fact that they are in desperate need of books for young adult readers. Often, when other teachers, parents, and students know that an educator is in need of books to build a library, the books will start to appear! So get the word out!

QUESTION 6: WHAT IF I DON'T HAVE ENOUGH COMPUTERS IN MY CLASSROOM?

This instructional method is flexible. Even if your classroom is not equipped with enough computers for each student, you can still use conversation journals to teach reading and writing. If you only have access to a few computers, you can distribute them to a small group and rotate them around the room a few times during the class period until everyone has at least ten minutes to write. The students who are not on computers are silently reading their choice books and getting ready to write, perhaps using their in-class writers' notebooks to record ideas.

When possible, bring your classes to the library or computer center where each student has their own computer. With more technology, the students can decide when to read and when to write and how much time to spend on each during this once-a-week lesson. Invite the librarian to co-teach with you to offer more students assistance with choosing books of interest and writing about them. Help your students feel comfortable in the library setting.

QUESTION 7: HOW DOES THIS METHOD WORK FOR STUDENTS WHO ARE STRUGGLING ACADEMICALLY, SOCIALLY, AND/OR EMOTIONALLY?

The Reading Conversation Journal, coupled with daily book talks and ten minutes of undisturbed classroom reading, was built with the reluctant, struggling reader in mind. Many of the student responses offered in this book are taken directly from the journals of students who came to eighth grade having never read a book on their own. Many of the responses contained in this text are from students who have repeatedly failed English, students who struggle with written expression, students who are not reading "at grade level," students with individualized education plans or 504s.

The RCJ gives *all* readers a chance to write about the things that they are reading in a way that might be more meaningful because they are selecting and reading the kinds of texts that they *want* to read.

For students who have struggled to read books on their own since they started grade school, suddenly having a large, diverse classroom library and a teacher who talks about books and genres on a daily basis might get them interested in reading again. Most reluctant readers at the middle level say that they have never had much of a chance to select their own book and that they really don't know what kinds of books are out there. They say that they do not know what type of book they like.

This method works because it helps readers first establish (or reestablish) their reading identity, and then allows for text discussions that develop and progress based on the needs of the reader at that particular moment. It is very low stakes, very student-centered.

It is important to note here that the RCJ is not a magic literacy elixir taken once a week to turn nonreaders into college-ready, lifelong lovers of books and literature. Most readers will respond with the help of the RCJ, but not all. Creating an environment where students are surrounded by diverse books and talking up five of those books per week and then giving students a chance to try out books and discover what they like and don't like with the help of a professional . . . well . . . it does kind of work like magic.

We must also note that with this conversation journal, we are hoping to nudge readers forward. Not that our expectations are low, but moving readers (and writers) forward is a *long* process that does not happen in one month or even one year. The growth of reading skills and habits takes multiple years of continued patience, nurturing, and care—decades of ongoing independent reading inside and outside of school, decades of conversation and discussion with professionals who coach and stimulate and remind and encourage and build on.

As we can see in the previous sections, one year of reading and conversation can make a big difference, but it is the continued application of the RCJ (year after year) that will change a reader into the lifelong literacy student that will shape society and the world for the better.

For struggling readers with little confidence and no idea as to what kinds of books they like, collaboration with special education teachers, librarians, and parents (and anyone else who wants to help) is key, and an integral part of the student growth and development. If a student is unwilling to read and select books on their own, then they will be unwilling to write in any meaningful way about text. Any adults who know the student and see them on a regular basis can help with the book-matching process, priming the reader at the start of the year with lots of high-interest, readable books that sync with passions and interests.

For reluctant readers, graphic novels and picture books work wonders at the start. Unfortunately, there is still a contingent of educational specialists (and parents) who view graphic novels and picture books negatively as appropriate reading material for middle level learners, arguing that these books are somehow less literary or less rigorous than "normal" chapter books. We won't delve into that battle here, but we will say that it is important to be flexible and inclusive when using the RCJ.

What works well for one student does not necessarily work well for another. Though we encourage all of our students to read both graphic novels and picture books, they might not appeal to *all* readers. For reluctant readers, though, more pictures and fewer words can be helpful (not to mention confidence-building). Rose (2017) offers middle-level teachers six picture book titles that continue to spark interest and passion among his eighth-grade readers.

Picture books should play a significant role in RCJ classrooms. Whether a student is revisiting a childhood favorite, taking a break after a particularly lengthy read (we love you Stephen King!), or experiencing a classic picture book for the first time (e.g., *A Chair for My Mother* [Williams, 2007]), picture books are often the spark that helps reignite the independent reading fire.

Don't forget, too, that *all* adults in the room must treat reading time with the utmost care and respect. It is *only* ten minutes a day, so everyone in the room reads. The only conferencing a teacher should do during that ten minutes is with a student who does not have a book (and the teacher should make it very clear that they are not happy that this exchange is interrupting their own reading time!).

QUESTION 8: HOW DO ONLINE READING CONVERSATION JOURNALS ALIGN WITH ELA STANDARDS AND EXPECTATIONS IN OUR FIELD?

Teachers sometimes ask us if we start our lesson- and unit-planning process first by looking at the standards and designing our instruction with each standard in mind, making sure we hit each standard. Or do we start with our practices (based on what our knowledge and experience tell us about how readers and writers learn best) and then go back to the standards to see how many we've met, which ones we've addressed, and which ones we've yet to use in our instruction, and then make adjustments?

Good teaching can happen both ways. But our preference is to begin with the practices that align most closely with what we know and have seen to work over time with our students, what it is we believe about how adolescents learn and grow in their literacy and language skills, what we're learning from the data we collect and from our ongoing professional reading. Interestingly, what we find when we proceed this way is that we are, in fact, addressing all standards set forth by our professional organizations. NCTE's (National Council of Teachers of English, 2019) recently revised definition of and position statement on independent reading state:

> [Definition:] Independent reading is a routine, protected instructional practice that occurs across all grade levels. Effective reading practices include time for students to read, access to books that represent a wide range of characters and experiences, and support within a reading community that includes teachers and students. Student choice in text is essential because it motivates, engages, and reaches a wide variety of readers. The goal of independent reading as an instructional practice is to build habitual readers with conscious reading identities. . . .

> [Position Statement:] Independent reading leads to an increased volume of reading. The more one reads, the better one reads. The more one reads, the more knowledge of words and language one acquires. The more one reads, the more fluent one becomes as a reader. The more one reads, the easier it becomes to sustain the mental effort necessary to comprehend complex texts. The more one reads, the more one learns about people and happenings of our world. This increased volume of reading is essential.

We trust our planning process when we arrive at this desired outcome again and again.

Next Generation ELA Standards

New York State has recently moved from Common Core to Next Generation ELA Standards (NYSED, 2017), with ELA arriving first, as usual. We always seem to lead the way for other core-area teachers because all lessons no matter the content are essentially literacy lessons, right? All lessons make use of literacy skills (reading, writing, listening, speaking, and viewing) to teach and learn disciplinary concepts. But this book isn't just for ELA teachers! You can share it with your content-area and special-area colleagues who are looking for a method that will bring more literacy into their curriculum, a method that will help their students use reading and writing as a means to understand, connect, and apply important content-specific and academic vocabulary and concepts.

Those who do not have a strong literacy background and may not be confident evaluating student reading and writing in more specific ways do not have to. There are no rules about how to modify this practice to fit any teacher's curriculum; it is a supportive method that can be done at any time with all students in all subject areas throughout all grade levels.

We do suggest, however, that teachers develop a clear plan before implementing Reading Conversation Journals, asking themselves what purpose this practice serves for them and for their students, what learning targets and content standards they are hoping to meet, what the parameters are around implementation and assessment.

Here are some questions you can ask yourself as you begin to implement your own Reading Conversation Journal activity:

- How often will students write?
- How often will I respond?
- Will it be graded? If so, why?
- How should it be graded? If not graded, what accountability measure will capture what I need to know in a fair and equitable (student-centered) way?
- In what ways will I ask them to write?
- In what ways will I respond?
- What texts will be available to students to read?
- Is my classroom library sufficient? How might I grow it in volume and diversity?
- How can I collaborate with my school librarian to better meet my goals and standards?
- Should all texts be self-selected, or should some be chosen by me?
- How will this activity fit in with the rest of my reading/writing lessons and curriculum?

The revised standards that all ELA teachers are required to address encourage holistic literacy practices such as read-alouds; independent, self-selected, pleasure reading; creative writing; and age-appropriate, high-interest text selections. See how many of them have been met simply by incorporating online Reading Conversation Journals one day per week into your ELA, content-area, or special-area classroom. When we analyzed the teacher-student conversations against each literacy practice, we realized that we are addressing all of them to varying degrees. As you read through these standards-based, lifelong literacy practices, consider three questions:

1. How do you currently plan and teach toward each lifelong practice?
2. Which practices might you want to put more time and energy into, and why?
3. What practices might you abandon or modify to make time for these new ones?

Lifelong Practices of Readers

1. Think, write, speak, and listen to understand.
2. Read often and widely from a range of global and diverse texts.
3. Read for multiple purposes, including for learning and for pleasure.
4. Self-select texts based on interest.
5. Persevere through challenging, complex texts.
6. Enrich personal language, background knowledge, and vocabulary through reading and communicating with others.
7. Monitor comprehension, and apply reading strategies flexibly.
8. Make connections (to self, other texts, ideas, cultures, eras, etc.). (NYSED, 2017)

Lifelong Practices of Writers

1. Think, read, speak, and listen to strengthen writing.
2. Write often and widely in a variety of formats, using print and digital resources.
3. Write for multiple purposes.
4. Experiment and play with language.
5. Analyze mentor texts to enhance writing.
6. Persevere through challenging writing tasks.
7. Strengthen writing by planning, revising, editing, rewriting, or trying a new approach.
8. Enrich personal language, background knowledge, and vocabulary through writing and communicating with others. (NYSED, 2017)

We know we're on the right track when we read the following position statement's definition and recommendations: "Leisure reading, also known as recreational reading, pleasure reading, free voluntary reading, and independent reading, is independent, self-selected reading of a continuous text for a wide range of personal and social purposes. It can take place in and out of school, at any time" (Leisure Reading Board Task Force, 2014, p. 2). In response to the general decline in leisure reading and the pressures to reduce the amount of leisure reading time in classrooms, three professional literacy education organizations (the International Reading Association, the Canadian Children's Book Centre, and the National Council of Teachers of English) have come together to take a stand on and support the value of independent reading at school and home. Their recommendations:

1. Students should choose their own reading materials.
2. The benefits to students' fluency, comprehension, and motivation from engaging in leisure reading are increased when teachers scaffold

school-based leisure by incorporating reflection, response, and sharing in a wide range of ways that are not evaluated. (Leisure Reading Board Task Force, 2014, p. 4)

The field of literacy education has set their expectations high, and the RCJ reading/writing activity reflects and affirms these best, lifelong practices. With the Reading Conversation Journal, teachers literally create a virtual one-on-one conversation with each of their readers.

QUESTION 9: HOW IS THE ONLINE READING CONVERSATION JOURNAL EVIDENCE-BASED?

The authors of this book followed a basic inquiry process from the onset, with our original question being, *How does the online Reading Conversation Journal help students become more independent readers and writers?* We weren't exactly sure how this student-centered approach to writing about reading would pan out, but we began developing a few hypotheses. Would students read during the ten-minute independent reading time each day? Would they write to the teacher each Friday about what they were reading? Would students become engaged with the reading? The writing?

Would the teacher have the time and energy to devote to responding to all of his students' thoughts and feelings about their reading on a weekly basis? Would this method yield the outcomes we desired: to create independent, engaged readers and writers who can choose and respond to a variety of texts in a variety of ways, and be well prepared for the literacy tasks required in high school and life? So many unanswered questions.

During data analysis, we began systematically reading, re-reading, and analyzing literally thousands of journal entries with accompanying teacher responses, coding them for emerging and recurring themes. Our themes sometimes surprised us and always energized us. They were aligning not only with ELA standards but also with our basic beliefs about the many authentic purposes literacy can serve in school and in life, and with our most fundamental beliefs about good literacy instruction.

We realized then that we were onto something that could contribute to the field of literacy and be replicated or adapted by teachers in most grade levels and in all content areas. The most robust themes eventually became the big ideas in parts II, III, and IV of this book. In each part, we noticed that we also had examples that reflected the diversity and range of learners in the class-room in terms of gender, background, prior knowledge and experiences, interests, social-emotional issues, and literacy levels and abilities.

Our book is a carefully selected subset of rich data culled from eighth graders' informal writings back and forth to their teacher about the books they read, what matters to them, and how they think and feel about what they read and write.

QUESTION 10: WHAT ARE THE OUTCOMES OF YOUR PROJECT?

The examples in this book provide evidence that our hunches were all correct. In fact, this one brief literacy activity yielded more positive results than we originally expected. These eighth graders *are* becoming more engaged, independent readers and writers in a multitude of ways when their teacher incorporates the RCJ.

Our argument throughout this book is that *we can meet the needs of all students* in our classroom, even when and especially when they come from a broad range of backgrounds, manifest a range of learning abilities, and speak different first languages. This holistic practice of allowing every student to choose from a variety of texts to read, then maintain a written conversation with the teacher about their text—all organized online in a safe, supportive environment—produced a richer dataset than we had imagined. Our data analysis has informed and continues to inform the practice; evidence continues to validate, inform, and support our belief system.

Our qualitative findings show clear evidence of student growth in terms of:

- strengthening their relationship with their teacher through trust, motivation, and confidence as readers and writers;
- greater self-awareness, resilience, and engagement as readers/writers;
- their ability to apply new definitions of what constitutes *text*;
- experimenting with new ways of responding to text;
- an increase in both reading and writing fluency; and
- an increase in both reading and writing volume.

Another unexpected outcome was quantitative in nature and reflects a goal any ELA teacher would desire. At the end of each quarterly marking period, this teacher administers a student self-assessment that, among other questions, includes a space for students to record the number of books they've read up to that point in time. This allows you to compare how individual students are doing, how each class is doing, and how all of your students are doing across all classes.

Wait for these impressive numbers! Each year since the Reading Conversation Journal has been a weekly priority and since this teacher has devoted the first ten minutes each day to self-selected independent reading, the number of total books read by students in five classes (roughly 110–120 students yearly) independently has increased dramatically: at the end of year 1, they had read over nine hundred books combined. In year 2, they had read over twelve hundred books combined—independently. And as of the writing of this sentence, during year 3, students will most likely have read upwards of two thousand books by year's end! These numbers speak for themselves.

There's more. These are only the choice books students read the first ten minutes of class, on Fridays, and outside of school. These totals do not include the whole-class texts and the many other types of reading and writing activities that engage students throughout the weeks and months of eighth grade. This evidence answers our original research question in more ways than we expected. When we give students time to read and time to write in school, encouraging choice and voice, we open up learning possibilities for all students that do not currently exist. We're eager to see what this total number is at the end of this year!

We know that teaching is an inherently metacognitive process in that we deliberately plan and use data collected in previous lessons (observations, discussions, reflections, formative assessments, writing samples, tests, quizzes, conferences, and so on) to inform our teaching in upcoming lessons. Data-driven instruction produces growth—both teacher growth and student growth. Our data is telling us that we need to continue with the RCJ.

How many of us have experienced a day, for example, when we will teach first period, reflect on and debrief the lesson second period (possibly with a trusted colleague), and by third period, we teach a stronger, revised lesson based on the reflective coaching conversation between periods? This should be happening on a regular basis in classrooms.

The process of reflection with a trusted colleague can propel a teacher in just a few short minutes from a good lesson to a great lesson, from a lesson that engages *some* students to a lesson that engages most or all students. After reflecting on our practice, we don't need to wait until the next day to change what didn't work well. We don't mention that we'll be sure to add it to our lesson next year when we teach this unit because, chances are, we'll forget to incorporate it. Rather, we revise on the spot, deleting the chaff and infusing new ideas that motivate and move students closer toward our learning targets.

In general, our online reading conversations serve as credible evidence that students are reading more and more widely and writing more and more fluently about their reading and developing their reading identities.

QUESTION 11: HOW DO YOUR TEACHING PHILOSOPHIES SHAPE YOUR LITERACY PRACTICES?

We have maintained an ongoing professional collaboration for about ten years now, mostly based on our common interest in, passion for, and beliefs about teaching and learning literacy. Our beliefs grow and change over time depending on many overlapping factors: our individual professional reading and writing (including following research in the field); our own personal reading and writing identities; designing and delivering professional development for literacy teachers and thinking about what these teachers teach us; and, probably most importantly, fifty-seven combined years of observing, teaching, reflecting on, and assessing thousands of readers and writers and hundreds of reading/writing lessons at many levels.

Each of these factors informs and shapes our beliefs, which in turn inform and shape our daily instructional decisions. Our lessons become more and more deliberately planned as our beliefs and practices become clearer and more aligned. This is what we refer to as instructional "integrity." It is planning by design, with a strong theoretical foundation and practical examples to support each theory *and* being open and flexible to the evolving nature of teaching and learning.

When we watch good literacy teachers, we become energized by the authentic, student-centered practices that offer students (and teacher) greater agency: rich and diverse literacy experiences that give readers and writers choice and options and time to think, which opens all of our minds to opportunities and possibilities rather than placing more rules, constraints, and restrictions on what and how we think, feel, and act.

Just as math teachers think aloud as they model how to solve certain kinds of problems, we believe good ELA teachers do the same with reading and writing problems. Strong literacy teachers read and write *with and to* their students and share their processes and products, and the response is powerful! Our theory is that free and voluntary reading has the potential to create lifelong readers, and so we devote class time for students to actually read and write and receive ongoing quality feedback on both. Students appreciate this.

We believe it's just as important to address the social-emotional well-being of students as it is to focus on academics, that when students feel good about what they're doing, they engage on a deeper level. Thus, we integrate activities that build classroom community so eighth graders feel a sense of belonging at a time in their lives when they truly need connection with and support from trusted, reliable adults. This is the data we rely on. This is evidence-based practice based on the application of theory to practice.

Fisher and colleagues (2016) found a strong connection between teacher-student relationship and student learning (effect size = .72). "If we want to ensure students read, write, communicate and think at high levels, we have to develop positive, trusting relationships with students, all students" (p. 13).

Let's remember that a teaching practice is only as good as the planning, implementation, and reflection that go into that practice. All good teaching moves through this metacognitive process, and without pre-planning and ongoing reflection, any practice (even a research-based practice) might just flop. This is one reason why a collaboration with another literacy profession-al is helpful. We have someone with whom to discuss challenges and suc-cesses, and to analyze our data. Looking at the same data or the same student, what we see is often different from what others see.

In a collaborative professional-learning partnership, we can more easily formulate and articulate our *whys* about the decisions we make every day in our classroom, developing our own personal philosophy of teaching literacy, and noticing how it evolves as we become more knowledgeable and skilled. Finding another ELA professional or two who can accompany you on this journey can be invaluable.

QUESTION 12: WHY ISN'T THIS SCENARIO HAPPENING IN MOST MIDDLE SCHOOL CLASSROOMS?

There are probably dozens of reasons that could be given for this question. We'll offer one. Some teachers are willing to leave themselves vulnerable to the possibilities that might occur when the decisions for and about students are not all made by the teacher ahead of time; by design, students and their strengths and interests and voices become a vital part of the curriculum and play important roles. But many teachers are not willing to do this.

When we have the courage to step away from formulaic, scripted lessons that often yield cookie-cutter student work, when our beliefs about what constitutes literacy learning are truly aligned with our practices, and when beliefs and practices continue to inform each other, unforeseen possibilities open up, including the willingness:

- to be vulnerable;
- to be fully present and honest with ourselves;
- to objectively analyze our craft;
- to be aware of each and every aspect of lesson planning, delivery, and assessment and how they impact kids;
- to be a mindful, reflective practitioner;
- to make needed changes (no matter how small) when the data suggests we make change; and
- to share our thoughts and feelings about what we do and why we do it on a regular basis with other trusted colleagues.

FINAL THOUGHTS

We want teachers and administrators to be inspired by this project. We want it to help bring about needed change in education and in the field of literacy instruction. We want it to embolden and support other teachers who are uncertain of what steps to take, which direction to take, how to engage themselves and their students, how to reignite their spark for teaching, how to engage students, which studies to read, which ones to believe in, which colleagues to emulate, which professional books to read, how to decide what's most important to teach and why, and where to spend the most instructional time.

Our job is big and multifaceted, and we should always remain mindful about the power teachers have to influence the children in our care.

We hope this book will also make a contribution to the field of teaching as it prompts teachers to begin or continue the conversation around the question *What* is *reading?* a question worthy of more of our time and attention—perhaps in our next book—a question we cannot ignore at a time when holistic language-learning practices are under close scrutiny. Suffice it to say that, like your philosophy of teaching literacy, your definition of *reading* and your definition of *writing* will greatly impact your instructional practices. We need to be aware of what it is we believe in, then keep watching and learning and studying and documenting as that belief system evolves over time.

Since many teachers ask us how and what this teacher teaches during the rest of his week (Monday through Thursday) supports and connects to the Reading Conversation Journal, we're already planning and thinking about our next book, which will focus on these practices, all holistic in nature, all focused on student engagement, all with big social-emotional *and* academic benefits to students and teachers.

We see ourselves as lifelong observers of our own craft, lifelong learners of teaching and learning—and encourage you to join us. We hear from teachers all over the country about how this way of journaling is helping their student readers and writers. We'd love to hear from you. Please send us some student responses, some feedback, or a question or two, once you begin implementing your own online Reading Conversation Journal.

Thank you for reading. Happy reading! Happy writing! Happy teaching!

Dan (drose@oswego.org)
Chris (christine.walsh@oswego.edu)
Website: https://sites.google.com/oswego.edu/roseandwalsh/home

References

Amazon. (n.d.a). *Best sellers in teen & young adult dance fiction.* Retrieved August 28, 2020, from https://www.amazon.com/Best-Sellers-Books-Teen-Young-Adult-Dance-Fiction/zgbs/books/10399752011

Amazon. (n.d.b). *Best sellers in teen & young adult historical fiction.* Retrieved August 28, 2020, from https://www.amazon.com/Best-Sellers-Books-Teen-Young-Adult-Historical-Fiction/zgbs/books/17437

Amazon. (n.d.c). *Best sellers in teen & young adult military historical fiction eBooks.* Retrieved August 28, 2020, from https://www.amazon.com/Best-Sellers-Kindle-Store-Teen-Young-Adult-Military-Historical-Fiction-eBooks/zgbs/digital-text/7006618011

Atwell, N. (2014). *In the middle: A lifetime of learning about writing, reading, and adolescents.* Heinemann.

Atwell, N., & Atwell Merkel, A. (2016). *The reading zone: How to help kids become skilled, passionate, habitual, critical readers.* Scholastic Inc.

Bailey, C. (2017). *The productivity project: Accomplishing more by managing your time, attention, and energy.* Crown Business.

Barnes & Noble. (n.d.). *Dancers & choreographers->biography->teen nonfiction: Books.* Retrieved August 28, 2020, from https://www.barnesandnoble.com/b/books/entertainment-biography-teens/dancers-choreographers-biography-teen-nonfiction/_/N-29Z8q8Z1lvw

Beers, K. (2012). *Notice and note: Strategies for close reading.* Heinemann.

Berkman, S. (2019). *A team of their own: How an international sisterhood made Olympic history.* Harlequin Books.

Calkins, L. (1994). *The art of teaching writing.* Heinemann.

Calkins, L. (2013). *Units of study for teaching writing.* Heinemann.

Calkins, L. (2020). *Teaching writing.* Heinemann.

Cambourne, B. (1993). *The whole story: Natural learning and the acquisition of literacy in the classroom.* Scholastic.

CASEL. (2019). *Collaborative for academic, social, and emotional learning.* www.casel.org

Casey, Amy. (n.d.). *Philosophy of education.* Universe as Text. Retrieved August 23, 2020, from www.universeastext.com

Chbosky, S. (1999). *The perks of being a wallflower.* MTV Books.

Clark, R. P. (2014). *How to write short: Word craft for fast times.* Little, Brown and Company.

Colby, L. (2015). *Road to power: How GMs Mary Barra shattered the glass ceiling.* John Wiley & Sons, Inc.

Conrad, J. (2014). *Heart of darkness.* CreateSpace Independent Publishing Platform.

Cormier, R. (2004). *The chocolate war.* Ember.

Cormier, R. (2007). *I am the cheese.* Ember.

Creech, S. (2010). *Hate that cat*. HarperCollins Publishers.

Dashner, J. (2009). *Maze runner*. Delacorte Press.

DiCamillo, K. (2015). *Because of Winn-Dixie*. Candlewick Press.

Energetiks. (n.d.). *A dancer's life* [blog]. https://www.energetiksblog.com.au

Farmer, N. (2004). *The house of the scorpion*. Atheneum Books for Young Readers.

Fecho, B. (2011). *Writing in the dialogical classroom: Students and teachers responding to the texts of their lives*. National Council of Teachers of English.

Fisher, D., Frey, N., & Hattie, J. (2016). *Visible learning for literacy, grades K–12: Implementing the practices that work best to accelerate student learning*. Corwin Press.

Frost, R. (1916). *The road not taken*. Henry Holt and Company.

Gallagher, K. (2009). *Readicide: How schools are killing reading and what you can do about it*. Stenhouse Publishers.

Gallagher, K. (2011). *Write like this: Teaching real-world writing through modeling and mentor texts*. Stenhouse Publishers.

Gallagher, K., & Kittle, P. (2018). *180 days: Two teachers and the quest to engage and empower adolescents*. Heinemann.

George, J. C. (1959). *My side of the mountain*. Scholastic Inc.

Gonzalez, J. (2017). *How to stop killing the love of reading*. Cult of Pedagogy [blog]. https://www.cultofpedagogy.com/stop-killing-reading

Hall, M., O'Hare, A., Santavicca, N., & Jones, L. (2015, April). The power of deep reading and mindful literacy: An innovative approach in contemporary education. *Innovacion Educativa, 15*(67). https://www.researchgate.net/publication/278017481_The_power_of_deep_reading_and_mindful_literacy_An_innovative_approach_in_contemporary_education/citation/download

Harris, T. (1989). *The silence of the lambs*. St. Martin's Paperbacks.

Hinton, S. E. (1967). *The outsiders*. Viking Press.

Ivey, G. (2014). The social side of engaged reading for young adolescents. *The Reading Teacher, 68*(3), 165–171.

Ivey, G., & Johnston, P. H. (2013). Engagement with young adult literature: Outcomes and processes. *Reading Research Quarterly, 48*, 255–275.

Kain, E. (2019, July 16). I have seriously mixed feelings about the end of 'Stranger Things" season 3 [updated]. *Forbes*. https://www.forbes.com/sites/erikkain/2019/07/16/i-have-seriously-mixed-feelings-about-the-end-of-stranger-things-season-3/#c4e5f4920b32

Kittle, P. (2013). *Book love: Developing depth, stamina, and passion in adolescent readers*. Heinemann.

Krashen, S. D. (2003). *Explorations in language acquisition and use*. Heinemann.

Krashen, S. D. (2011). *Free voluntary reading*. Libraries Unlimited.

Krashen, S. D. (2019, August 18). How kids become readers. *Los Angeles Times*.

Krathwohl, D. R., Bloom, B. S., & Masia, B. B. (1964). *Taxonomy of educational objectives: The classification of educational goals. Handbook II: Affective domain*. David McKay Company Inc.

Lear, P. (2012). *The Battle of Oswego*. WCNY. http://www.wcny.org/education/war-of-1812/the-battle-of-oswego

Leisure Reading Board Task Force. (2014). *Leisure reading*. Joint position statement of the International Reading Association, the Canadian Children's Book Centre, and the National Council of Teachers of English. http://www.literacyworldwide.org/docs/default-source/where-we-stand/leisure-reading-position-statement.pdf

Linnihan, M. (2016, April 26). Dance is not a sport: Here's why it's so much more. *Odyssey*. https://www.theodysseyonline.com/dance-is-not-sport

Marchetti, A., & O'Dell, R. (2018). *Beyond literary analysis: Teaching students to write with passion and authority about any text*. Heinemann.

McNeil, G. (2013). *Ten*. Balzer Bray.

Melville, H., & Walcutt, C. C. (2003). *Moby Dick*. Bantam Books.

Mikaelsen, B. (2002). *Touching spirit bear*. HarperCollins Publishers.

National Council of Teachers of English. (2019, November 7). *Statement on independent reading*. https://ncte.org/statement/independent-reading

New York State Education Department (NYSED). (2017). *NYS Next Generation Learning Standards*. www.nysed.gov

New York State Education Department. (2019). *Student support services: SEL*. www.p12. nysed.gov

Nhat Hanh, T. (2017). *Happy teachers change the world: A guide for cultivating mindfulness in education*. Parallax Press.

Obama, M. (2018). *Becoming*. Crown.

Owl City. (2016, November 7). *Fireflies (official live video)*. YouTube. https://www.youtube.com/watch?v=I6NSS-CC93o

Palmer, P. (1998). *The courage to teach*. John Wiley and Sons.

Palmer, P. J. (2017). *The courage to teach*. Jossey-Bass.

Panofsky, C., Eanet, M., & Wolpow, R. (n.d.). *Literacy and the affective domain: Three perspectives*. Retrieved August 25, 2020, from http://www.americanreadingforum.org/yearbook/yearbooks/01_yearbook/html/03_Panofsky

Park, B. (1983). *Operation dump the chump*. HarperCollins Publishers.

Park, B. (1988). *The kid in the red jacket*. Yearling.

Park, B. (1996). *Mick Harte was here*. Yearling.

Park, B. (1997). *Skinny bones*. Yearling.

Park, B. (2002). *Don't make me smile*. Yearling.

Park, B. (2002). *The graduation of Jake Moon*. Aladdin Paperbacks.

Paulsen, G. (1987). *Hatchet*. Bradbury Press.

Poe, E. A., Parini, J., & Bernard, A. (2008). *The complete poetry of Edgar Allan Poe*. Signet Classics.

Reading Rockets. (2012). *Building reading stamina*. https://www.readingrockets.org/article/building-reading-stamina

Reed, G. A., Reed, C., & Reed, G. (2000). *Fort Ontario, NY: Guardian of the North*. Arcadia.

Rose, D. (2017). *Six picture books that even a middle schooler will love*. Parent.com. https://www.parent.com/6-picture-books-that-even-a-middle-schooler-will-love

Rosenblatt. L. (1994). *The reader, the text, the poem*. Southern Illinois University Press.

Rowling, J. K. (2007). *Harry Potter and the deathly hallows*. Scholastic Inc.

Sachar, L. (2019). *Sideways stories from Wayside School*. HarperCollins Publishers.

Salinger, J. D. (1945). *Catcher in the rye*. Little, Brown and Company.

Schwalbe, W. (2017). *Books for living: Some thoughts on reading, reflecting, and embracing life*. Vintage Press.

Serravallo, J. (2017, May). Dropping everything to read? How about picking some things up? *Voices from the Middle, 24*(4), 24–27.

Shusterman, N. (2016). *Challenger deep*. HarperCollins Publishers.

Smylie, M. (2014). *The barrow*. Pyr.

The Decemberists. (2014, November 24). *Make you better (official)*. YouTube. https://www.youtube.com/watch?v=Yb8oUbMrydk

The Decemberists. (2020, August 16). In *Wikipedia*. https://en.wikipedia.org/wiki/The_Decemberists

thomyorke74 [username]. (n.d.). *The Decemberists—down by the water*. YouTube. https://www.youtube.com/watch?v=qR9DjdMrpHg

Vizzini, N. (2015). *It's kind of a funny story*. Hyperion.

Wallace Foundation. (2017, March). *Navigating SEL from the inside out*. www.wallacefoundation.org

Walsh, C., & Rose, D. (2015). Designing relevant vocabulary warm-ups. *Voices from the Middle, 23*(1).

Williams, V. (2007). *A chair for my mother*. Greenwillow Books.

Williams, W. C. (2018). *The red wheelbarrow and other poems*. New Directions Publishing Corporation.

Woodson, J. (2016). *Brown girl dreaming*. Puffin Books.

Young, A. (2019, July 14). How I wrote 'Fireflies.' *Songwriting Magazine*. https://www.songwritingmagazine.co.uk/how-i-wrote/fireflies-owl-city

About the Authors

Daniel Rose has been teaching middle school English Language Arts in Oswego, New York, for two decades now. He has a BA in elementary education, a master of arts in English, and K–9 permanent teacher certification. He has presented his work at local, regional, state, and national literacy conferences, including the Central New York Reading Council, the New York State Reading Association, and the NCTE Annual Convention. Dan has published numerous professional articles on literacy and teaching middle-level reading and writing both online and for *Eureka Street* and *Teachers and Writers* magazines and NCTE's journal, *Voices from the Middle.* Dan lives in Oswego, New York, where he continues to teach, write, and coach varsity golf, with the support of his wife, Kelly, and three kids: Sebastian, Sydney, and Ellie.

Christine Walsh is a visiting assistant professor in the Department of Curriculum & Instruction, School of Education, State University of New York at Oswego, where she serves as co-director of the annual Oswego Writing Institute; facilitates professional development school university/school partnerships through Team Sheldon; teaches undergraduate and graduate education courses; and supports school teachers and administrators as an instructional specialist and literacy coach/consultant. A former high school English teacher, Chris holds certifications in K–6 elementary education, 7–12 English education, and school building/district leadership, and earned her doctorate from the Department of Reading and Language Arts at Syracuse University. Chris enjoys a busy yet peace-filled life in Baldwinsville, New York, with her husband, Brian; son, James; and beloved golden retriever, Bailey.

Made in the USA
Middletown, DE
16 November 2020

24211309R00102